Images of America
JEFFERSON COUNTY
WISCONSIN

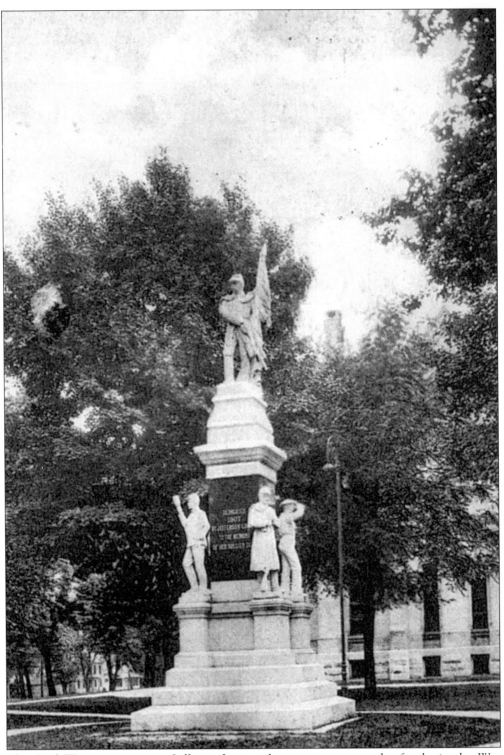

The Civil War monument in Jefferson honors the many veterans who fought in the War between the States from 1861 to 1865. The monument was dedicated in 1907.

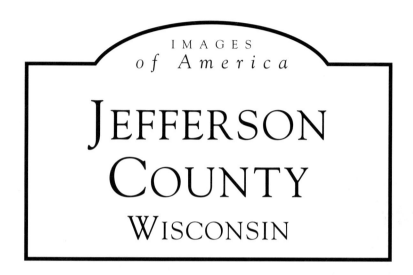

IMAGES
of America

JEFFERSON COUNTY
WISCONSIN

Jefferson County Historic Alliance
Text by W.F. Jannke III, President

Copyright © 1999 by Jefferson County Historic Alliance.
ISBN 0-7385-0307-X

Published by Arcadia Publishing,
an imprint of Tempus Publishing, Inc.
2 Cumberland Street
Charleston, SC 29401

Printed in Great Britain.

Library of Congress Catalog Card Number:

For all general information contact Arcadia Publishing at:
Telephone 843-853-2070
Fax 843-853-0044
E-Mail arcadia@charleston.net

For customer service and orders:
Toll-Free 1-888-313-BOOK

Visit us on the internet at http://www.arcadiaimages.com

Contents

Introduction		7
1.	Aztalan, Lake Mills, Milford, and Cambridge	9
2.	Cold Spring and Hebron	31
3.	Concord and Ixonia	41
4.	Fort Atkinson and Sumner	53
5.	Jefferson	67
6.	Johnson Creek	83
7.	Palmyra	95
8.	Rome and Sullivan	107
9.	Waterloo	115
10.	Watertown	119
Acknowledgments		128

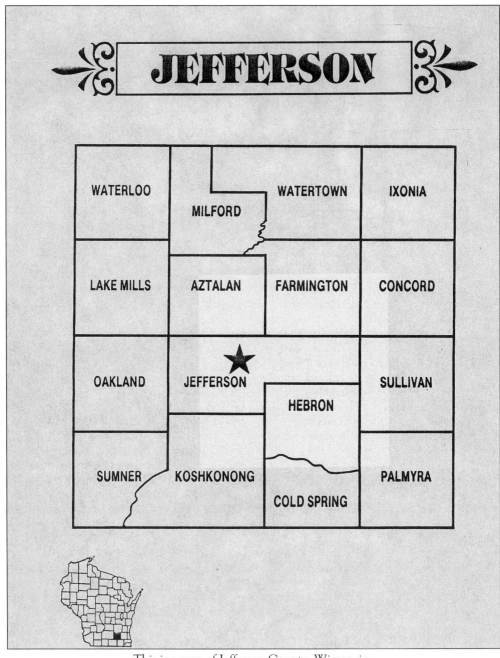

This is a map of Jefferson County, Wisconsin.

INTRODUCTION

As we take our first hesitant steps forward into the new century, it is only right and proper that we pause to look back on all that we and our forebears have accomplished over the past 160 years.

The first Yankee settlers began to arrive in what is now Jefferson County in 1835 and 1836. Prior to their arrival, Native-American tribes such as the Ho-Chunk and Pottowatomis claimed this area. Even earlier, members of the so-called "Mound Builder" race were settled here before the time of Columbus. While all published histories trace the story of the county to 1836, the county's roots go back considerably further into the murky mists of time.

Traces of these early residents are few and far between. Apart from an intaglio mound in the Fort Atkinson area and the ceremonial burial mounds preserved at Aztalan State Park and other places in the county, the signs of early man in this area are virtually nonexistent.

Evidence of European occupation, however, is very much present. From the county's ten historical societies and their museums, to the many cities and towns with their distinctive buildings, residents and visitors to Jefferson County are reminded on an almost daily basis of the history of this area.

Who were these early settlers? The first to arrive were Yankees, mainly from New England. The Yankees sought to make this area like their hometowns in the East. Towns with names like Concord, Rome, and Watertown began to spring up, complete with New England customs and values. These settlers were followed by the Irish and Germans who brought with them culture and traditions that helped to make the county unique. Today, almost every ethnic group is represented, thus making the county a perfect example of a cultural melting pot.

Early pioneers were attracted to this area because of its abundant land, with its fertile soil and running rivers, teeming with fish. In a short time, agriculture became the main industry in the county. In many areas it still remains the main focus.

Once the power of the Rock, Crawfish, and Bark Rivers had been harnessed by a series of dams, milling became an important industry. Sawmilling became prevalent, and logs soon choked the Rock River as they made their way down to large distribution points in Janesville and Beloit. Sawmills made it easier to build, and as a result, frame dwellings began to dot the landscape.

Flour milling followed soon afterwards. It became easier for farmers to have their grain ground into flour, thus reducing their dependence on the big city for flour. Flour milling opened a cash market for grain, thus enabling farmers to buy more. By the mid-1800s virtually every town had a flour mill, with the largest of these mills being the Milford Mill, with seven millstones.

But agriculture still held sway with wheat being the major cash crop here until the mid-1860s. Then, as a result of bad harvests, insect infestations, and a nation-wide decline in prices, the wheat market in Jefferson County bottomed out. However, by then a new agricultural industry began to take root in Jefferson County: dairying.

Men like Governor William D. Hoard and others took a little thought of industry and elevated it to one of worldwide importance. With the founding of the Wisconsin Dairymen's Association in 1871, the future of dairying was assured. This group introduced new ideas and procedures that streamlined the industry, and by the 20th century (and for many years after that), Jefferson County became the leader of the dairy industry.

Education also played an important role in the make-up of the county's character. Such important educational firsts as the first kindergarten in America, founded in Watertown in 1856, and the first free textbooks in the state bear witness to the county's commitment to the educational betterment of its children. From one-room rural schoolhouses to state-of-the-art learning centers, Jefferson County is still in the forefront.

Religion has also played a part in the make-up of the residents of the county. The first dominant religious group in the county were the Methodists, who had circuit-riding ministers preaching throughout the area. They were followed by Catholics, Congregationalists, Baptists, Presbyterians, Episcopalians, and, with the arrival of the Germans in the mid-1840s, Lutherans. In 1850, there were only 19 churches in all of Jefferson County. By 1870, there were 51 churches, and today there are over 100 churches for residents to choose from.

But what of the future? Since the 1960s, farmland has slowly been disappearing, along with historically significant farm buildings and barns. Urban development threatens small communities throughout the county. And it isn't just the rural landscape that is changing. Urban centers and Main Streets are rapidly losing their importance as business centers jostle for position along well-traveled state highways. As the century has changed so, too, has the complexion of Jefferson County.

It was therefore felt that a reminder of what the county once was, was needed. Hence, the book you have before you. It is hoped that the pictures arranged in this book serve to remind you, the reader, resident and former residents of the county, of what it was that brought people to this area in the first place.

An early settler once wrote to his parents that he was sure St. Peter wouldn't allow him into Heaven when he died because he lived in Jefferson County when he was alive and therefore he was already in Heaven. We think so, too.

One
AZTALAN, LAKE MILLS, MILFORD, AND CAMBRIDGE

The towns of Aztalan, Lake Mills, Milford, and Cambridge make up a group of some of the oldest places in the county. The date of the founding of these towns go back to the very beginnings of the county.

Aztalan was founded in 1836 by Thomas Brayton, Jared F. Ostrander, Stephen Fletcher, and others. Prior to the arrival of white settlers, Native Americans of a culture far more advanced than that of the simple woodland tribes had built a stockaded village on the west side of the Crawfish River. The tribes had flourished there for perhaps 200 years before the arrival of European settlers. The town takes its name from this early tribe, which many believe was the founder of the Aztec culture in South America.

Situated at the junction of two well-traveled roads, Aztalan, it was felt, was destined for greatness. It quickly became the largest city in the county. But when the railroad passed it by, it became a virtual ghost town. Today, approximately 1,472 people live in the township.

Lake Mills also traces its roots to 1836, the year when Captain Joseph Keyes came to the area and laid claim to the lands that now encompass the city. Like many Wisconsin settlements, the town's early industries were related to agriculture, some of which gained national importance. In 1841, Ann Pickett started a small dairy cooperative, the first dairy cooperative in the United States. The Phillips family, which arrived in 1849, is credited with starting the first commercial creamery in Wisconsin. All of this happened in Lake Mills.

Diverse business enterprises and a love of fun have made Lake Mills a wonderful spot to live. With its lakeside parks, multiple boat landings, and public beaches, Lake Mills has remained a source of enjoyment in southeastern Wisconsin.

The towns of Milford and Cambridge have a long history. Milford, as its name implies, was noted for its mills and, at one time, had one of the largest in the county, the old Milford Mill with seven millstones. When this mill burned down in 1883, the town gradually lost businesses and citizens to nearby Lake Mills. Today, it is a small crossroads town.

Cambridge has always been noted for its location. Situated on scenic Lake Ripley, Cambridge has long been a popular vacation spot for tourists seeking to "get away from it all." Among the many well-known residents of the village were Arthur Davidson, the co-founder of the Harley-Davidson motorcycle company, and Ole Evinrude, the inventor of the first outboard motor. Today, Cambridge is still a popular tourist haven. It is home to several fine gift shops as well as the Rowe Pottery Works. There is something for everyone in Cambridge.

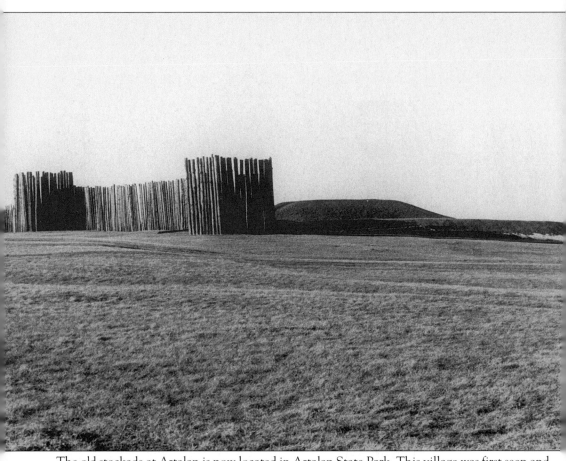
The old stockade at Aztalan is now located in Aztalan State Park. This village was first seen and claimed by Timothy Johnson, later founder of Watertown, and sold to Judge Nathaniel Hyer in 1836.

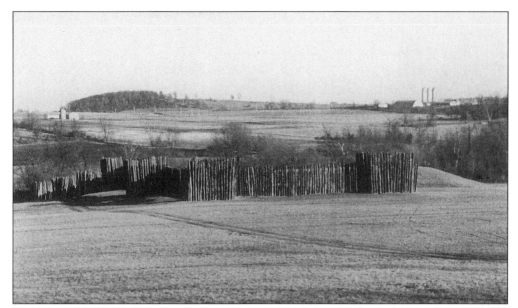

The "Ancient Village" site was originally a tribal village that housed two large pyramidal mounds, houses, and cornfields. The village was first seriously studied and surveyed by Increase Lapham, state geologist, in 1850.

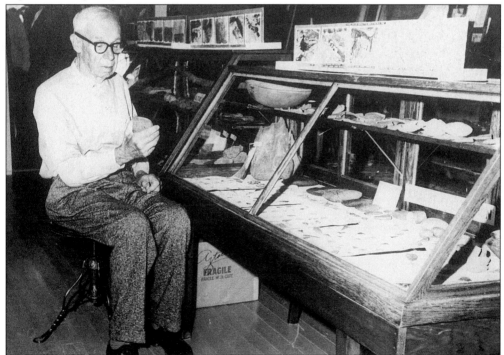

Since the 1940s, there has been a serious effort on the part of individuals, such as the late Albert Kracht, seen here, to preserve the site of the ancient village. Kracht was the first curator and is shown with the Aztalan Historical Society's collection of Native American artifacts. In 1968, he was given a special award of merit from the State Historical Society of Wisconsin for his efforts in helping to preserve this rich archaeological site.

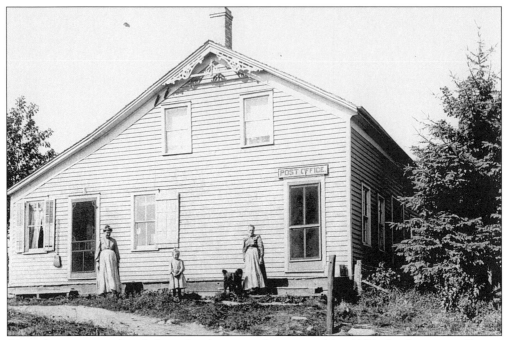

Once the town was founded, settlers began to flow in, and by 1837, the first post office in Aztalan was established. Nathaniel F. Hyer served as the first postmaster. This shows the post office as it looked in the 1890s.

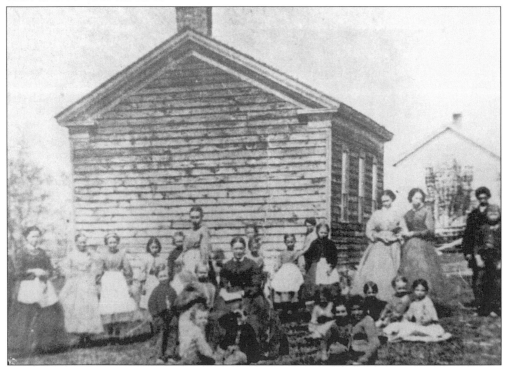

The first Aztalan school, made of wood, stood in the south public square. It was later replaced by a brick building in 1850.

The Aztalan Baptist Church was built in 1852 with Milwaukee brick. It is the only remaining building left of pioneer Aztalan. Today, it serves as the Lake Mills-Aztalan Museum.

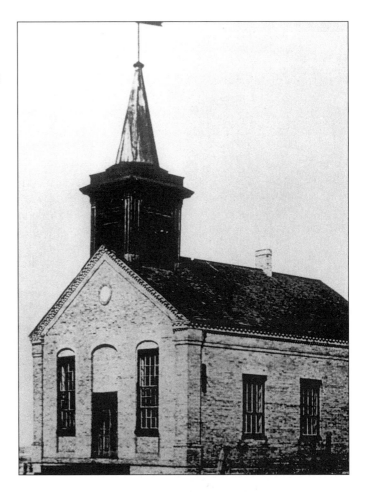

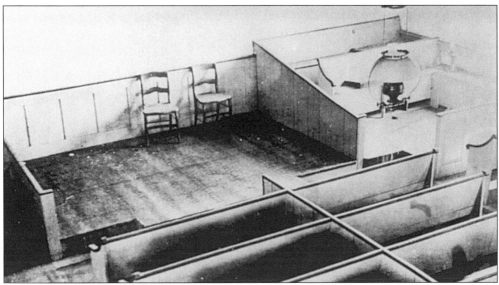

The interior of the Aztalan Baptist Church shows the simplicity of the settings.

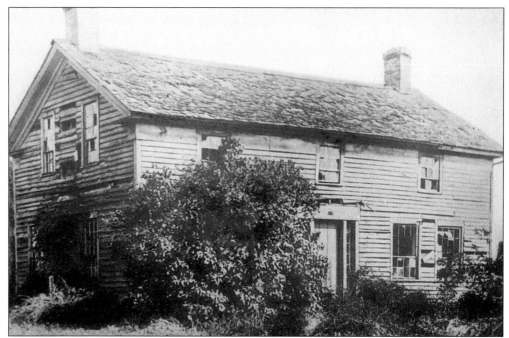

The Ancient City House was Aztalan's first hotel. It was built in 1840 to accommodate the ever-increasing flow of settlers. County judge Thomas Brayton also used the building from 1843 to 1846 to hear probate cases.

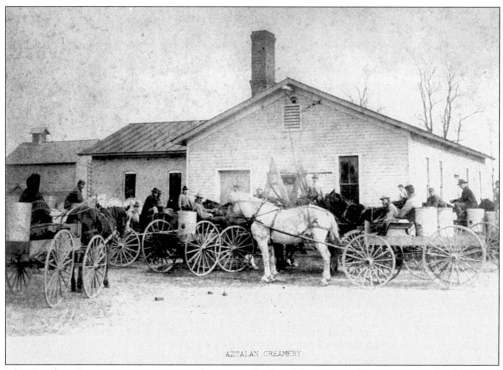

The Aztalan Creamery was a source of revenue for local farmers in the vicinity in the 1800s.

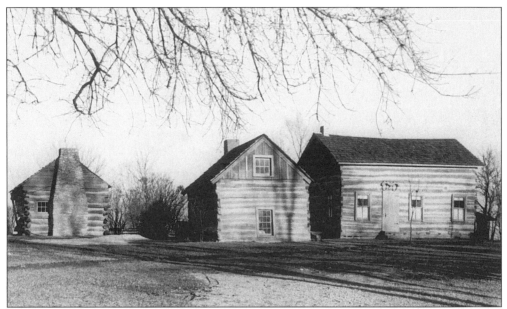

The Aztalan museum grounds are pictured here with its restored cabins. The three, all built in the 1840s, include the Pettey cabin, the two-story Zickert house (on the extreme right), and the Loom house. Today, one can view these cabins and get a sense of what it was like to be in a pioneer town. In addition, the museum also boasts a granary, a log cabin church, and a schoolhouse, in addition to the old Baptist Church, which houses a collection of artifacts relating to Aztalan when it was the county's largest town.

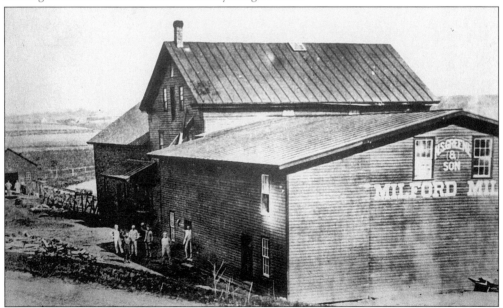

The Old Milford Mill was one of the best known in the county. The flour and grist mill was built in 1845 by Norman Pratt and acquired a year later by Nathan S. Greene. This was considered one of the top mills in Jefferson County and was powered by the Crawfish River. The turning point in Milford's history came in 1883 when the mill was destroyed by fire, thus reducing the town to a pale shadow of its former greatness.

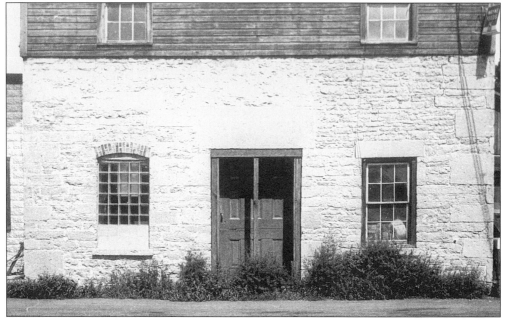

The century-old Hooper's Mill, near Lake Mills, was built of native materials obtained nearby. Erected in 1854 by the Hooper family, the mill remained in operation until 1948, when Alvin Vehlow and Raymond Kowski bought it. Standing on Rock Creek near the outlet of Rock Lake, the mill produced as many as 70 barrels of flour a day.

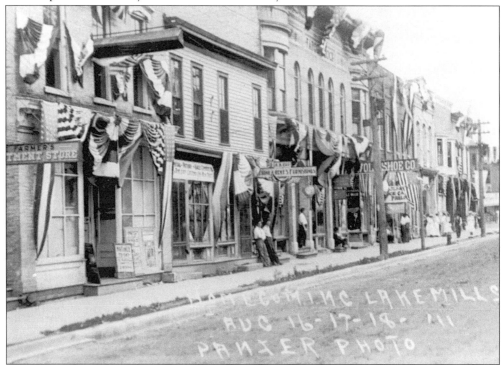

Lake Mills is one of the older towns in the county. Shown here is a view of Lake Street in 1911 when the annual homecoming was in progress.

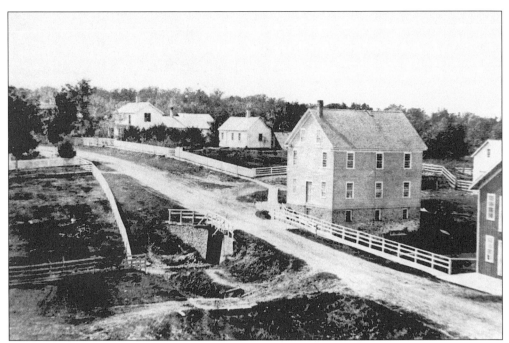

The Keyes Sawmill, one of the oldest structures in Lake Mills, is shown in this picture. It is the second building on the right and was built in 1839 by Captain Joseph Keyes, the first settler of Lake Mills. The lumber the mill produced was a great help to the early settlers. In the fall of 1842, Keyes opened a grist mill that used the same waterpower as the sawmill.

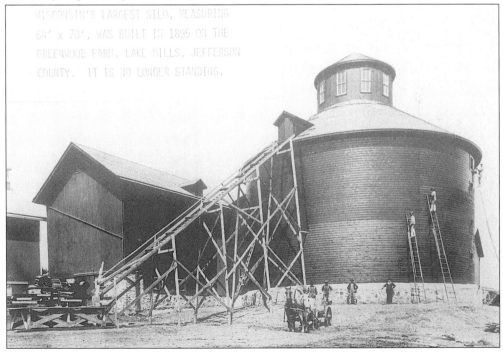

Wisconsin's largest silo, measuring 64 by 70 feet, was built in 1895 on the Greenwood farm in Lake Mills. It is no longer standing.

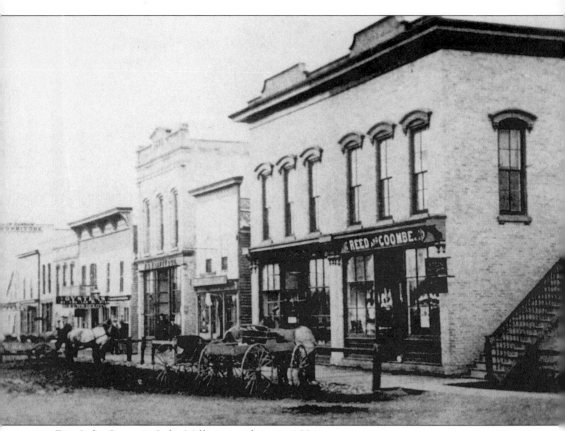
East Lake Street in Lake Mills is seen here in 1884.

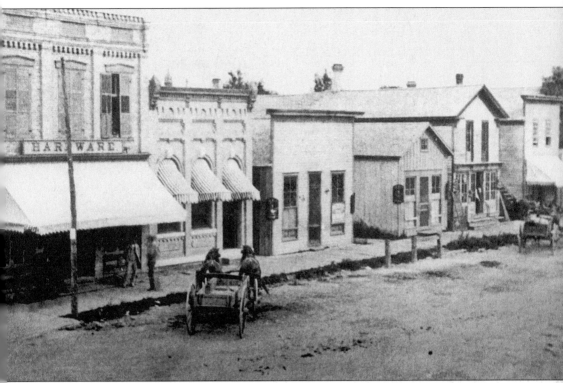

North Main Street in Lake Mills is pictured here in 1884. At this time a history noted that Lake Mills was "a village of 700 inhabitants without a foot of cement walk or a rod of hard-surfaced road or a street light worthy of the name."

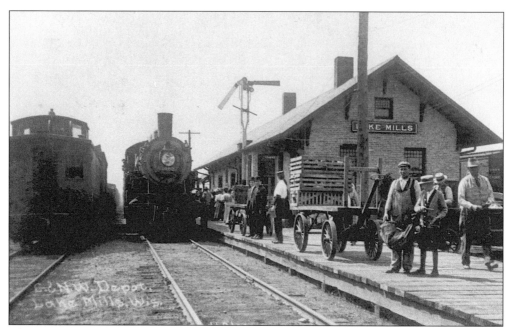

The Chicago and Northwestern railroad station in Lake Mills was built in 1890. The railroad added the connection when Lake Mills began to be a popular summer resort town and had several growing industries.

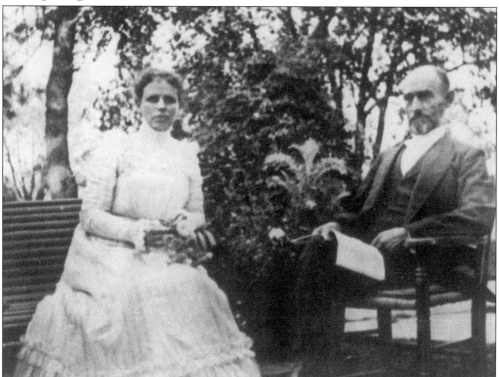

This is a portrait of one of the first families of Lake Mills, Mr. and Mrs. Robert Fargo. Among the many industries the Fargos were involved were banking, milling, and dairying.

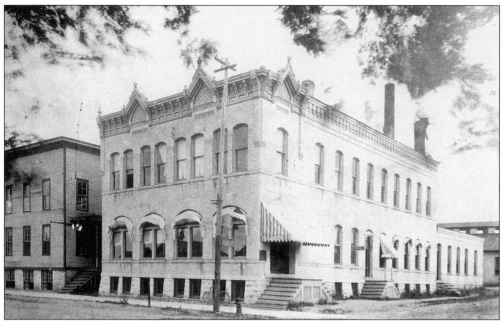

The F.B. Fargo Dairy Supply Company was founded in 1870. Today, this is the Lake Mills municipal building. The original Dairy Supply Company became a subsidiary of the St. Regis Paper Company.

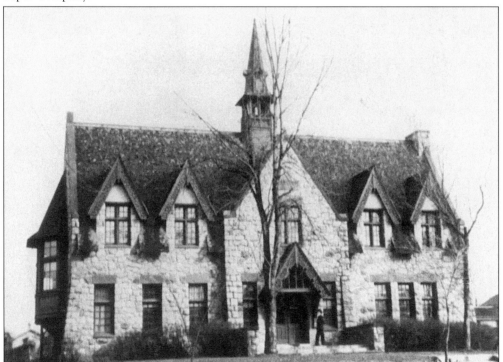

The L.D. Fargo Library was designed by George Ferry, who also designed the State Historical Society building. The Fargo Library was built from granite gathered from the vicinity. The building was formally dedicated in August 1902.

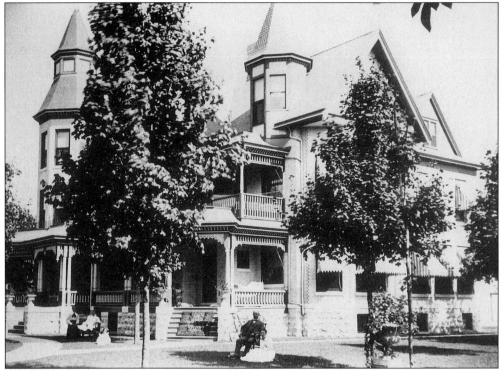

The Enoch J. Fargo mansion was built c. 1895. This mansion is now the Fargo Mansion Inn, a bed and breakfast.

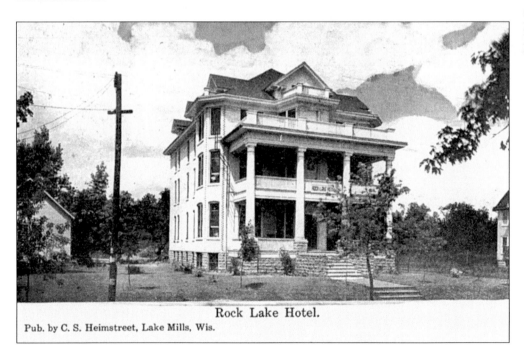

The Rock Lake Hotel is now known as the Bayberry Inn. This was one of the better hotels in Lake Mills and even boasted steam heat as early as 1885.

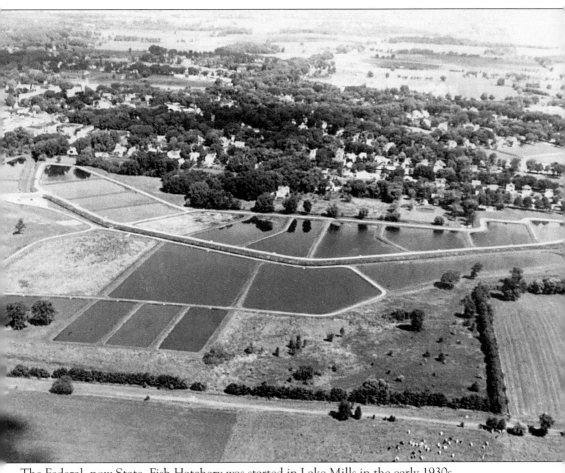
The Federal, now State, Fish Hatchery was started in Lake Mills in the early 1930s.

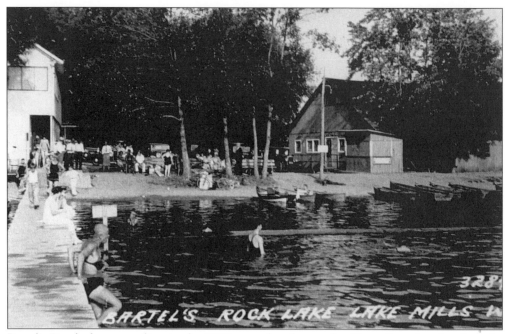

Bartel's Beach dance pavilion in the 1930s was the place to be. One of two beaches in Lake Mills, Bartel's Beach is a free beach that has played host to thousands of visitors yearly.

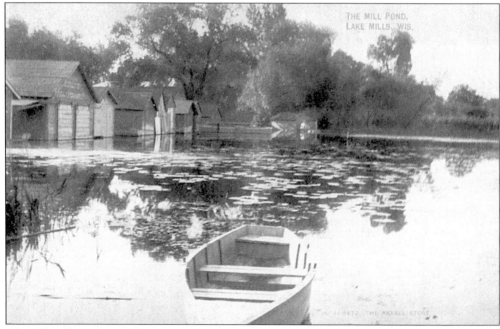

The old mill pond in Lake Mills is seen here c. 1910. Water sports have always been a noted attraction in Lake Mills.

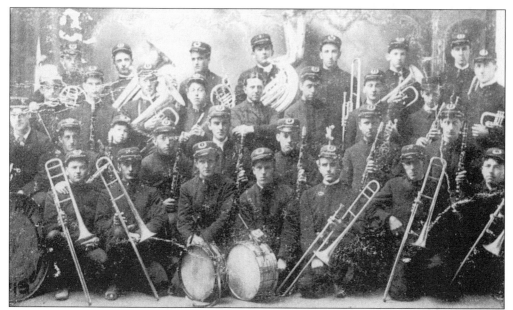

The Lake Mills Concert Band had this picture taken c. 1890s. Music has been popular in Lake Mills since 1844, when the first band was founded. Fred Ray, one of the leaders of the Lake Mills band also organized the first University of Wisconsin band in 1882.

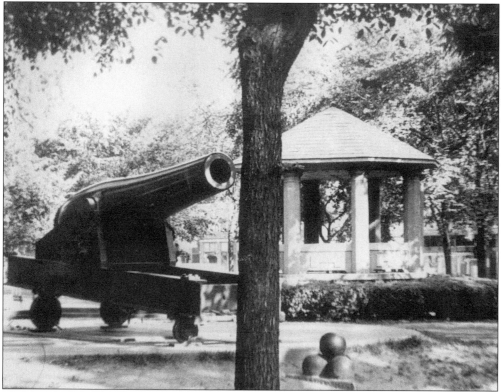

The City Park in Lake Mills was the site of weekly band concerts. The band shell was built in 1911, and the cannon was added during World War I. This picture was taken in 1936.

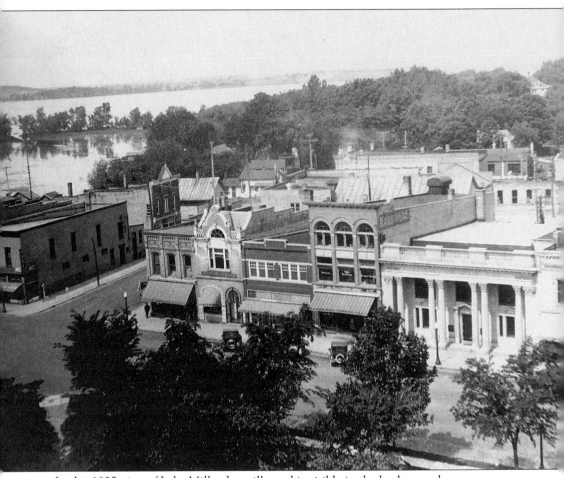
In this 1925 view of Lake Mills, the mill pond is visible in the background.

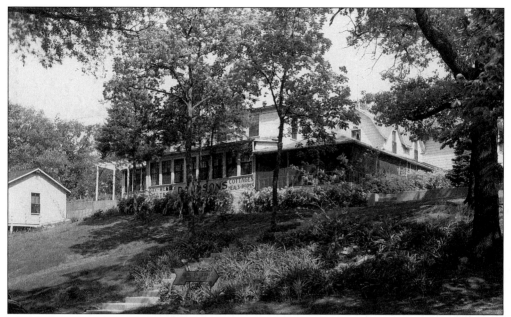

The Arthur Davidson cottage in Cambridge is located on Lake Ripley. Arthur Davidson was one of the pioneers in the motorcycle industry.

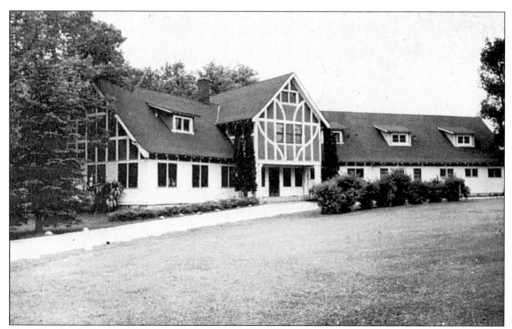

The Cambridge-Lake Ripley area has long been a haven for vacationers. In order to cater to these out of towners, several hostelries opened in the area. One such place was the Lake Ripley Country Club, shown here in the 1930s.

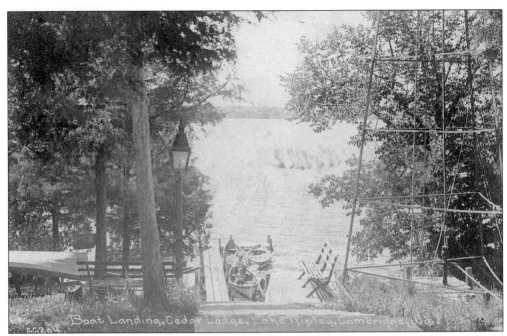

A boat landing at Cedar Lodge in Cambridge is the subject of this view. Cedar Lodge, like so many lodges and inns, flourished long ago in Cambridge. It was on a boat like the ones pictured here that Ole Evinrude came up with the idea for the first outboard motor.

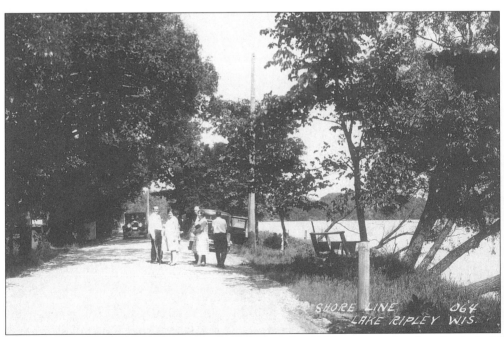

The shoreline along Lake Ripley in Cambridge in the 1920s was tree-lined and relatively undeveloped. It is no wonder that people were drawn to this area.

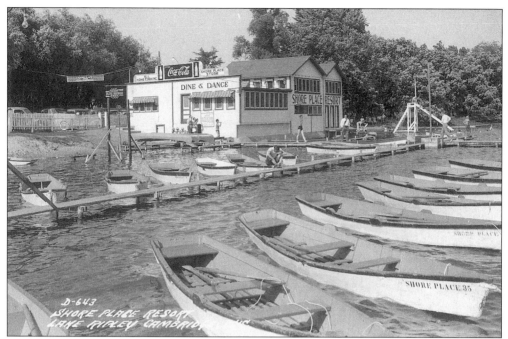

Boating and all manner of water sports have always been popular in Cambridge. This 1940s image shows the Shore Place Resort, which catered to those who enjoyed boating on beautiful Lake Ripley.

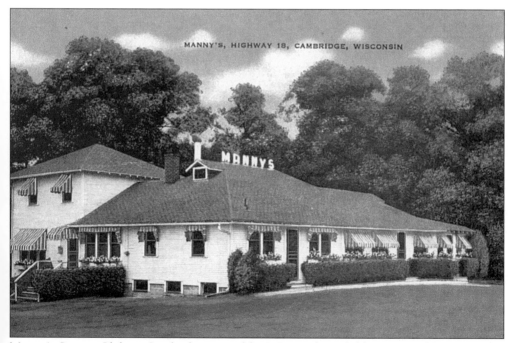

Manny's Supper Club in Cambridge, owned by E.B. Haubenschild, is pictured here in 1947. This restaurant specialized in dinners, lunches, and had a complete bar service.

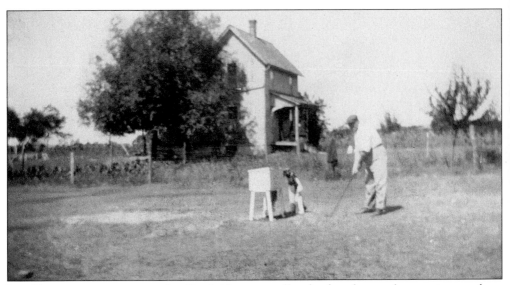

In addition to water sports, the Cambridge area offered other forms of recreation, such as golfing. Here, Thomas Kees, a summer resident, is shown playing a round of golf.

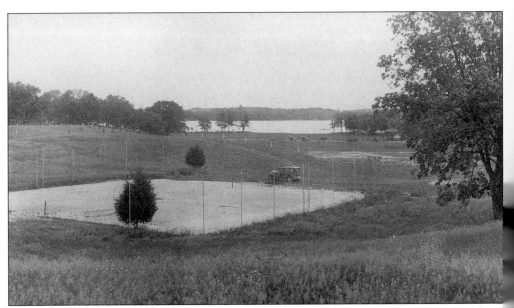

The community park was located along Lake Ripley in Cambridge. Many games of golf and baseball were played here.

Two
COLD SPRING AND HEBRON

Perhaps the oldest settlement in Jefferson County is the Hebron and Cold Spring area. Hebron was founded in 1835 by members of the Rock River Claiming Company, headed by Solomon Juneau. They erected a mill at this site, called the Bark River Mills, and a town sprung up around it.

In 1837, Cyrus Cushman built the first framed house in 1843 and erected a dam and sawmill on the Bark River. He floated lumber down the Rock River to Illinois and also had a run of stone for grinding meal.

By the 1850s, Hebron was the second largest city in the county. Between 1865 and the early 1870s, Hebron boasted two mills, one large bedstead factory (for making bed frames), a post office, a creamery, two general stores, two shoe shops, a repair shop, two blacksmiths, a potash factory, a brick yard, a milliner's shop, two hotels, and two saloons. But, like Aztalan, when the railroad didn't come through the town, village growth gradually was curtailed. Today, Hebron is a small crossroads hamlet.

Cold Spring, named for a spring of cold, pure water, was founded by Alexander Henderson in 1837. Among the more interesting facts regarding this settlement include a marker which tells of Abraham Lincoln losing his horse during the Black Hawk War in 1832. Cold Spring was also the boyhood home of Governor George W. Peck, author of *Peck's Bad Boy* and other works of humor. The well-known Northwestern Indian photographer Edward S. Curtiss was also born here in 1868.

But like so many other towns, the railroad did not come through Cold Spring, and its people moved to other towns that offered jobs. Stores closed, and the factories that once existed in the little hamlet, such as the coffin factory (you weren't considered properly buried unless you were laid out in a Cold Spring coffin one history boasted), ceased operations until those people living in the town became employed and did their business in nearby communities. Today, Cold Spring, like Hebron, is a crossroads hamlet.

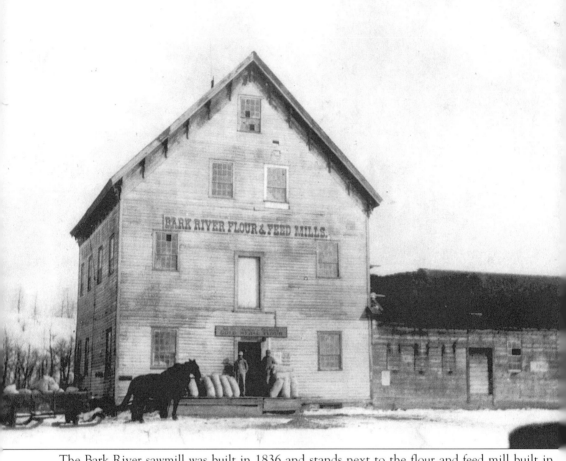

The Bark River sawmill was built in 1836 and stands next to the flour and feed mill built in 1852 by Joseph Powers. The sawmill was first staked out in 1835 and went into operations in 1836. It was the first mill of its kind in Jefferson County.

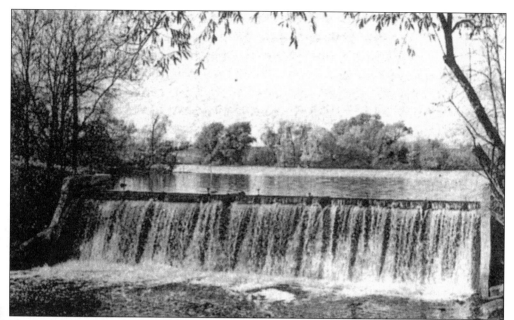

The Hebron Dam, built in 1836, was the first dam in the township. It was dismantled by an order from the Department of Natural Resources in 1996.

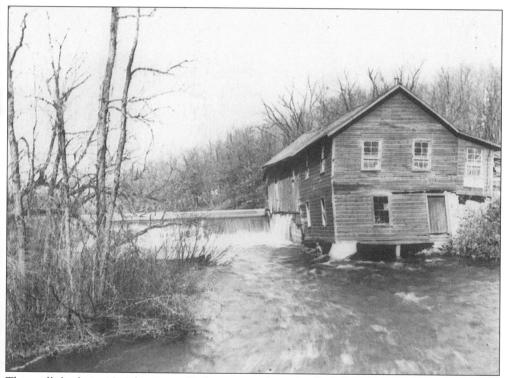

This mill, built in 1843 by Cyrus Cushman, stood on the Bark River until 1954, when it was destroyed by fire. The lumber sawed here was rafted down the Bark and Rock Rivers to Rockford and other Illinois towns for $4 per thousand feet.

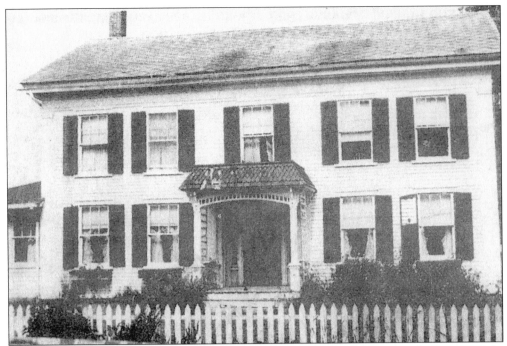

The Cushman house was built in 1843 by Cyrus Cushman. His first home was built in 1837. In 1843, upon completion of his saw mill, he built this house, which was the first frame house in the township. It was still being lived in by descendants of the original builder in 1999.

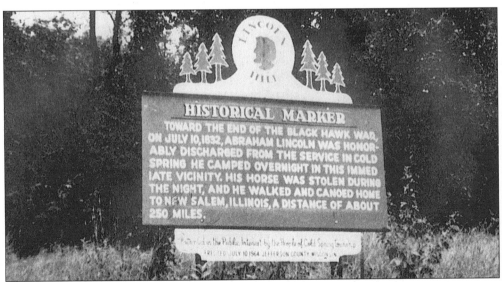

On July 10, 1832, Abraham Lincoln, while serving in the Black Hawk War, lost his horse in Cold Spring and had to walk home 250 miles to New Salem. Today, a sign marks the spot where Lincoln lost his horse.

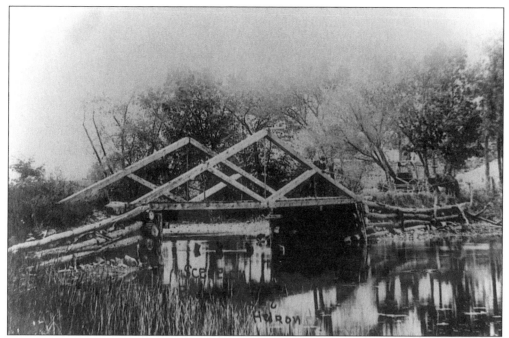

This wooden bridge, built in Hebron and spanning the Bark River, was built in the 1850s and was used until it was replaced with an iron bridge.

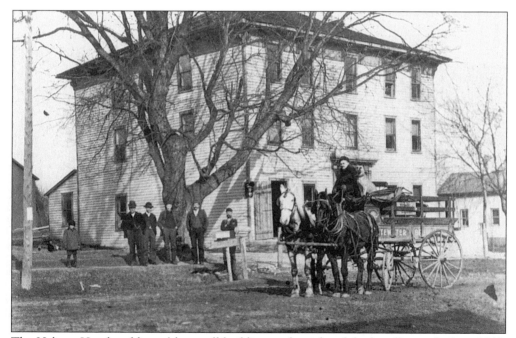

The Hebron Hotel and barn (the small building to the right of the hotel) were built in 1846. The brewery wagon in the foreground is from the Whitewater area. The hotel no longer exists.

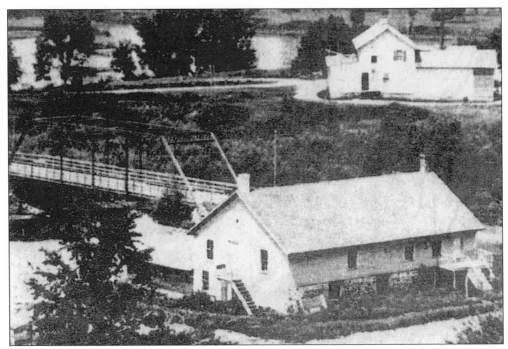

The Hebron Cheese Factory is seen here in 1885. A butter factory is in the rear, and the iron bridge that replaced the original wooden one can also be seen in this photograph. By 1878, more than 500,000 pounds of cheese were being produced in Hebron.

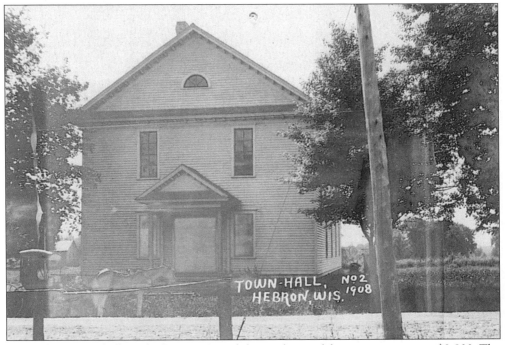

The Hebron town hall was built in 1902, and the total cost of the construction was $3,800. The interior was covered with patterned metal sheeting. Since 1981, the building has been home to the Town Hall Museum, the headquarters of the Bark River Woods Historical Society.

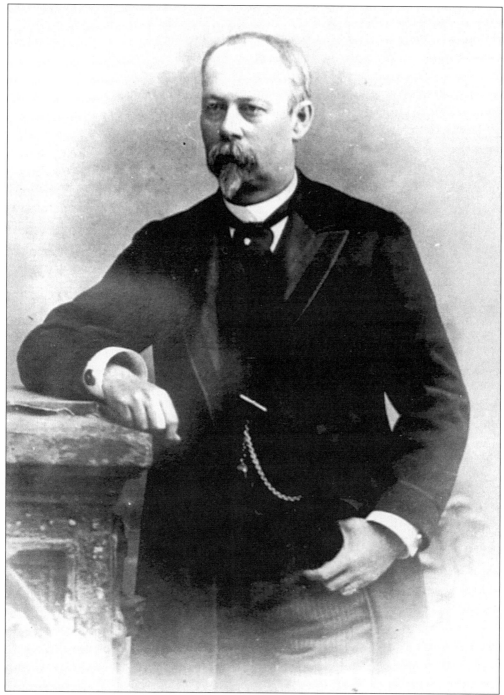

George W. Peck was born in Cold Spring and attended school there. He later worked for several newspapers and was the author of the humor classic *Peck's Bad Boy*. He also served as governor of the State of Wisconsin from 1891 to 1895.

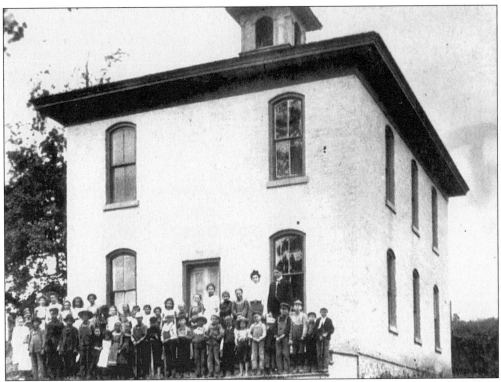

Hebron School District No. 3 was built sometime before 1854. It was in use until the 1950s and is currently a private residence. This view shows the school in the early 1900s.

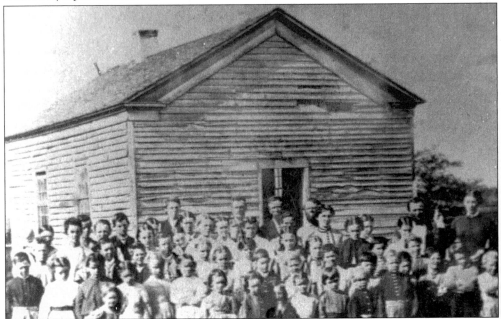

This picture shows the Tamarack View School in Hebron Township, c. 1880s. It was built on what is today's State Highway 106, east of Fort Atkinson, and no longer stands. This was typical of many early one-room rural schools.

Stone School in Cold Spring Township was built in 1869. The building was constructed of native stones found in the area. The school is now used as a community center and the headquarters of the Stone School 4-H Club.

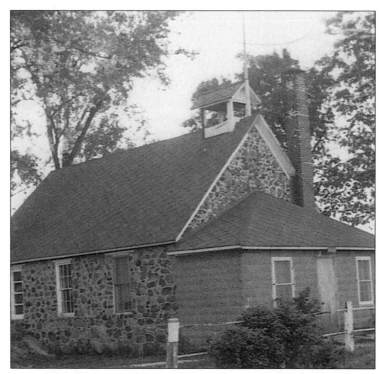

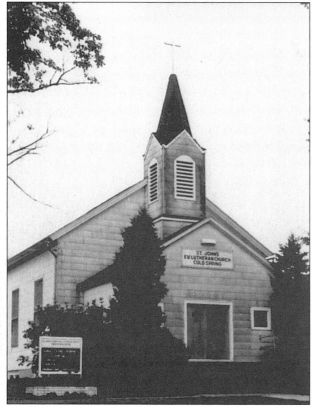

St. John's Evangelical Lutheran Church in Cold Spring was built in 1862 and, with some exceptions, still looks basically the same as is did at that time.

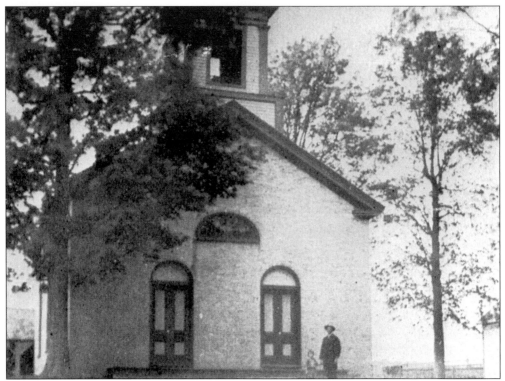

The first Hebron M.E. Church was built in 1856 and destroyed by fire in 1898. The congregation was first organized in 1839 and celebrated its 160th anniversary as a congregation in 1999.

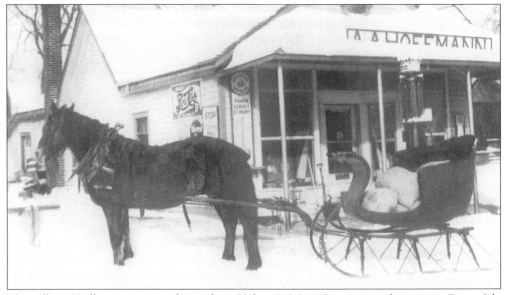

The Albert Hoffman store was located on Hebron's Main Street, now known as Green Isle Drive. This general store was a popular spot for many years and is currently a private residence. This photo dates to 1942.

Three
CONCORD AND IXONIA

The history of Concord dates back to February 12, 1841, when townships seven and eight, north of range 16, were separated from the town of Watertown to form the town of Union. On January 21, 1846, Union Township divided into two separate towns, called Concord and Ixonia. The two towns took separate paths to future development. The railroad would be routed through Ixonia, providing opportunities for commerce and industry. The town of Concord, however, remained a rural township with a focus on agriculture and dairy farming.

The town of Concord was a central stopping point between Milwaukee and Madison and the Wisconsin Stage Lines route along the old territorial road. Concord grew from a population of 725 in 1850, to 1,627 by 1870. By the turn of the century, Concord was a growing farming community, with a town hall, a post office, a general store, schools, churches, a sorghum mill, a barber shop, a creamery, and cheese and butter factories. But the town's chief claim to fame is that the parents of the famous author of the *Little House On The Prairie* series of books, Laura Ingalls Wilder, lived here and were married here.

The town of Ixonia was named by pulling letters from a hat. It remains the only town in the United States that bears this name. The first town meeting was held on April 21, 1846.

Statistics reveal that there were once many sawmills, five icehouses, eight cheese factories, a stockyard, and a railroad depot in operation at one time in Ixonia. The railroad first reached the town in 1855, and in 1888, a depot was built. It closed in 1966 and was razed three years later. Today, all have vanished except for the cheese factories, which have been converted into private homes.

The people of Ixonia count themselves as citizens of a progressive township with roots that began over 150 years ago. Presently there are 2,895 people living in the township.

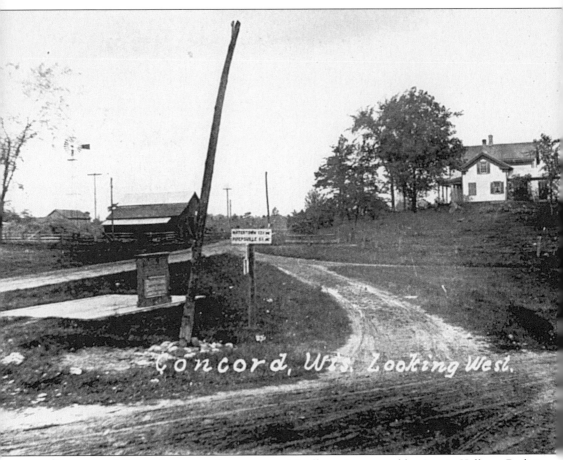

The town of Concord stagecoach stop was originally an inn owned by Austin Kellogg. Built in the early 1840s, it was razed in the early 1990s.

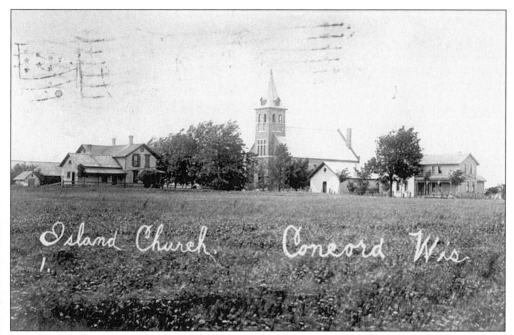
This is an early view of St. Stephen's Lutheran Church, also known as the Island Church. St. Stephen's was founded in the 1850s.

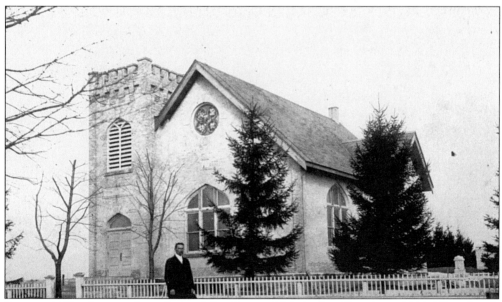
Reverend Klenskey stands in front of the Concord Methodist Church, c. 1916. This church replaced the old Concord Methodist Church, which had a tall steeple that was struck by lightning, causing a fire that destroyed the entire church in 1915.

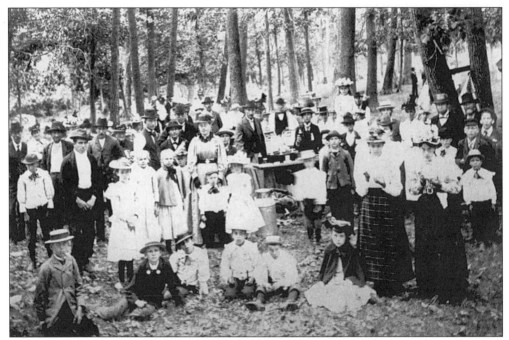

This Fourth of July picnic was held by Methodists from the Concord area in the early 1900s. Celebrations such as this were widely attended by the citizens of Concord, whether they were Methodist or not.

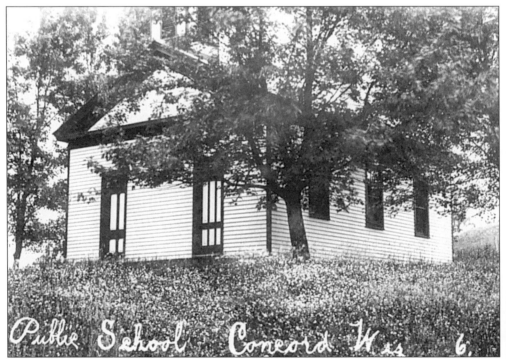

The Concord Center School, pictured here c. 1915, is today the site of the town hall.

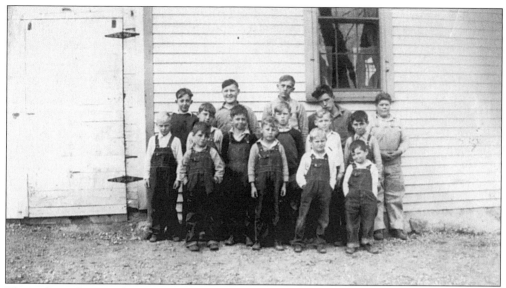
The male students of the Concord Center School are pictured here in 1935.

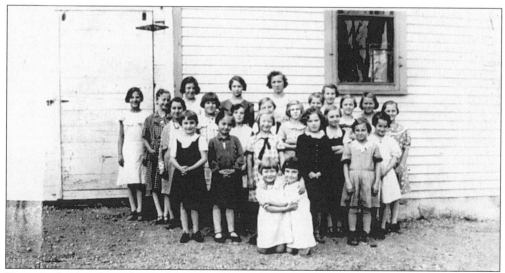
Here are the female students of the Concord Center School in 1935.

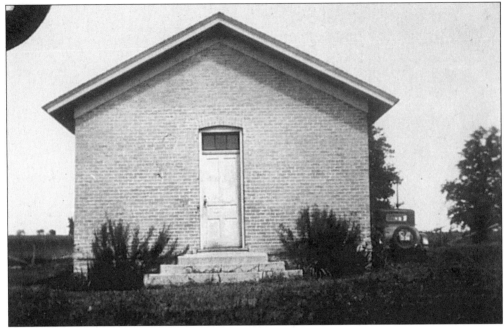

The Highmound School in Concord, c. 1932, like so many other rural school buildings, ceased to operate in the 1950s. Note the teacher's car parked on the right. Today, the school is a private residence.

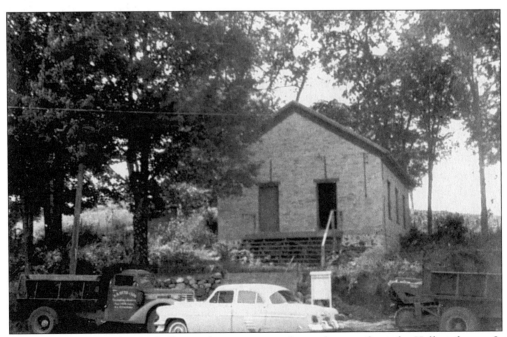

The original Concord town hall, seen here, was once located across from the Kellogg house. It was torn down many years ago.

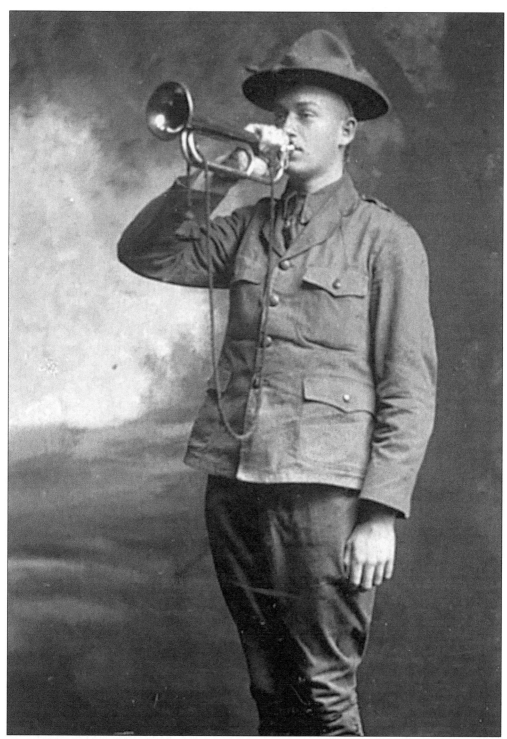

Concord sent many men to the front in World War I. One such man was Chester Ingersoll, who was a bugler. Ingersoll was a descendant of Lorenzo Ingersoll, who came with his family in the 1840s and settled in Concord.

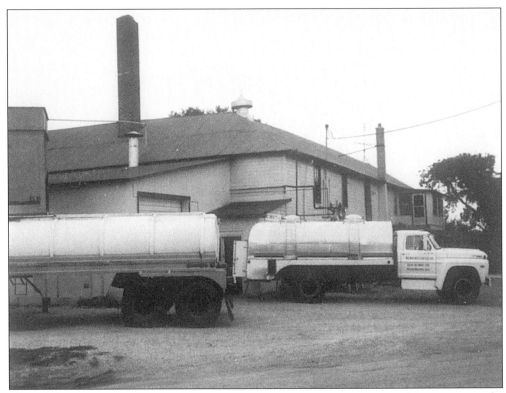

The Concord Cheese Factory was located on East River Road and was owned for many years by the Ness family, who were of Swiss heritage. The building is now used as a residence.

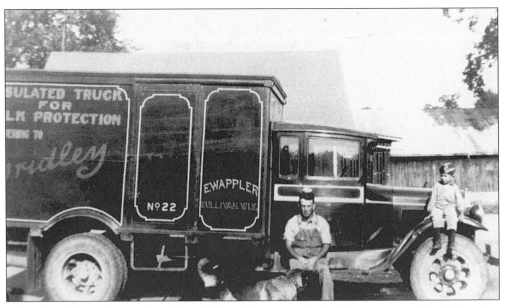

This photo shows Concord residents Palmer Zastrow and Lyle Wappler, son of Earl Wappler. Palmer Zastrow was a driver for Earl Wappler, who delivered milk for the Gridley Company in the 1930s.

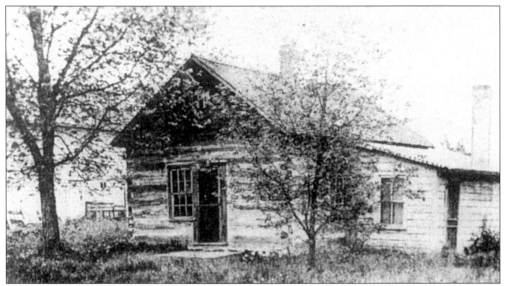

This photo shows the Piper log cabin, built by Benjamin Piper and his two sons Harrison and Elijah. The cabin stood in Ixonia for many years and was one of the first homes in the township.

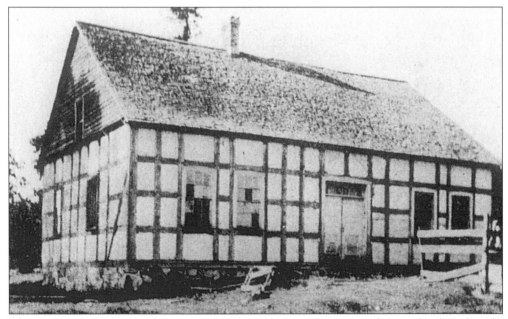

The German influence can be seen in this Ixonia home. This is a good example of "Fachwerk" or a half-timber home. Emigrants often replicated building styles they were familiar with from their homeland.

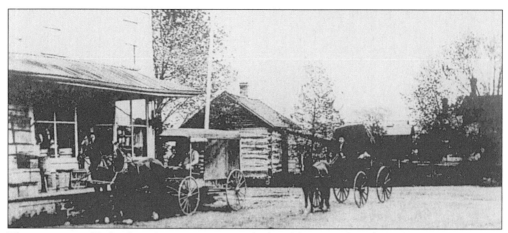

This is a view of Rabenhorst's grocery store with the old Piper cabin in the background. Stores like this were the lifeblood of the community and served as a meeting place for settlers as well as a place to buy goods.

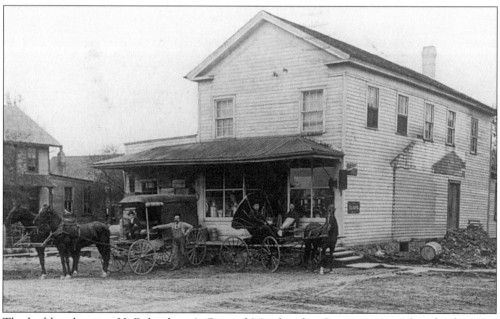

The building housing H. Rabenhorst's General Merchandise Store was moved to this location from nearby Vicksburg. It has undergone several changes and today is a cycle shop. It is considered to be the oldest building in Ixonia.

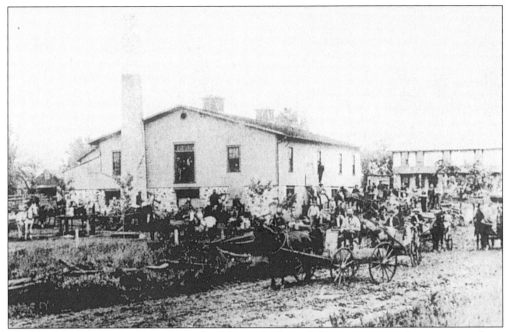

The Ixonia Creamery was established in the early days of the community. At one time, there were three cheese factories in Ixonia. Today, the old creamery houses equipment for excavating and septic system services.

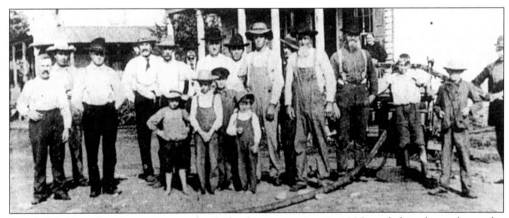

Ixonia bought a hand pumper on wheels for fire protection in 1905, and this photo shows the men who manned the pump in 1906. The first volunteer company was officially organized in 1931 and was incorporated in 1944. In 1955, a new firehouse was built, and currently, the town owns two fire engines.

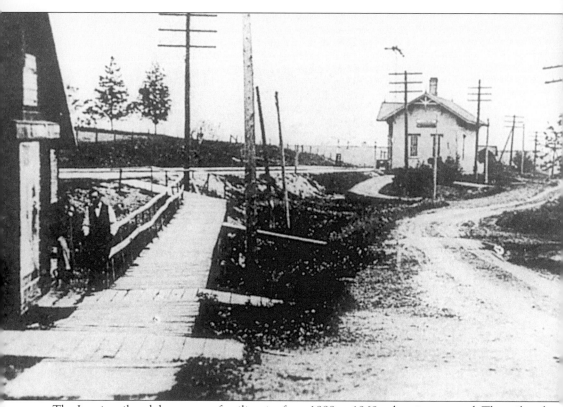
The Ixonia railroad depot was a familiar site from 1888 to 1969, when it was razed. The railroad made its first appearance in Ixonia in 1855.

Four
FORT ATKINSON AND SUMNER

Fort Atkinson has its origins shortly after the end of the Black Hawk War of 1832, which marked the last Indian war east of the Mississippi in American history. Settlers journeyed to this area in search of rich soil, a welcome change from the poor rocky soils of their native New England. Modern streets and buildings still honor some early settlers, such as Dwight Foster, Aaron Rankin, Milo P. Jones, and Lucien B. Caswell. The name of the city is taken from General Henry Atkinson, a notable figure in the Black Hawk War.

The earliest settlers were Dwight Foster and his family who came here in 1836 and built a log cabin. They began feeding and housing other travelers as they passed through the pioneer village. In 1841, Foster built the first frame house and later served as the postmaster, opened the first hotel, and operated a ferry service across the Rock River.

Another notable resident of the city was Milo P. Jones. Jones was a surveyor who laid out much of Jefferson County. His son Milo II established the Jones Dairy Farm in 1898. Their production of pork sausage began in the family kitchen, but as the result of a national advertising campaign in 1904, their product gained world-wide recognition.

But the most important resident to come out of Fort Atkinson was William Dempster Hoard. Hoard is the man who is generally considered the "father of dairy farming" in Wisconsin. A newspaper man, agriculturist, and politician, he founded *Hoard's Dairyman*, a national dairy publication in 1885, and also served as governor of the State of Wisconsin.

Fort Atkinson prides itself on preserving its community heritage. Two historic districts preserve the architectural history of the city and the Hoard Historical Museum maintains a large archive of documents, photos, and items relating to the rich history of the community.

Nearby is the town of Sumner, the smallest township in the county. It contains only 17 square miles and was created by a division of the town of Koshkonong in 1858. Notable early settlers there include Thure Kumlien, famed pioneer naturalist, and Sterling North, author of *Rascal* and *So Dear To My Heart*.

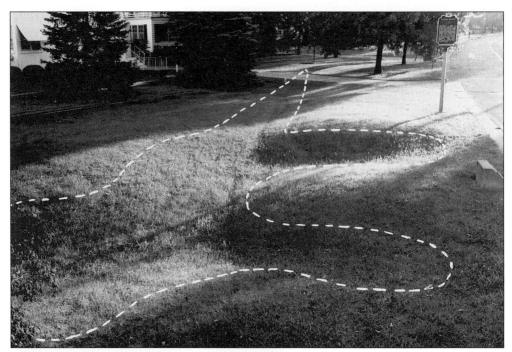

On Highway 106, just west of downtown Fort Atkinson, a historical marker identifies the only complete surviving intaglio in the world. Native Americans of the Effigy Mound Culture probably excavated it for ceremonial purposes about 1000 A.D. It was first "discovered" in 1850 by the surveyor Increase Lapham. Lapham recorded the existence of nine other panther intaglios in Southeastern Wisconsin, but Fort Atkinson's intaglio is the only one left. In 1970, it was listed on the National Register of Historic Places.

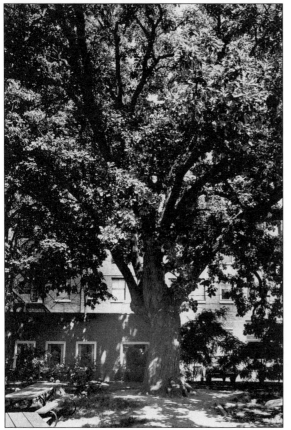

The oldest tree in Fort Atkinson is a huge burr oak tree on the grounds of the Congregational Church. It was used as a marker by pioneers traveling along the army trail to Fort Cosconong, the name of the old stockade that later became the site of Fort Atkinson.

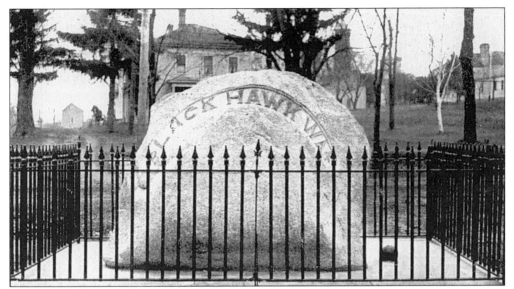

The Black Hawk War monument in Fort Atkinson was placed on the site of the old stockade commanded by General Henry Atkinson during the Black Hawk War. The marker was erected by the Fort Atkinson Daughters of the American Revolution (DAR).

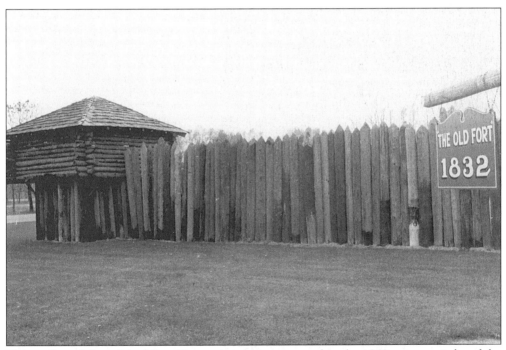

This replica of the original Fort Cosconong was constructed in the 1960s as a reminder of the historic origin of Fort Atkinson. During the 1970s, it was used as a backdrop for the dramatic Black Hawk Pageant, which was a reenactment of the tragic events of the Black Hawk War of 1832. It is now the site of a Buckskinner's Rendezvous every May.

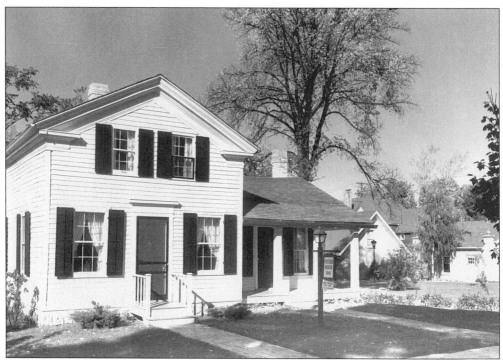

Built by fellow pioneer Charles Rockwell for the princely sum of $2,000, the Foster House was the first frame house constructed in Jefferson County. Dwight and Almira Foster were the first settlers in Fort Atkinson, arriving in 1836. This two-story, five-room home, built in 1841, was their home until Dwight's death in 1870. In 1969, it was given to the Fort Atkinson Historical Society and was moved to its current location on the grounds of the Hoard Historical Museum.

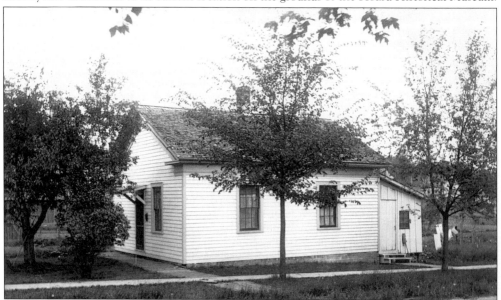

Fort Atkinson's first school was opened in 1839. The teacher, 14-year-old Jane Crane, instructed six pupils. Both the teacher and the location would change every year until pioneer carpenter Charles Rockwell finally built this schoolhouse in 1844.

A Vermont native, Milo Jones first came to Fort Atkinson in 1835 as a government surveyor. Impressed with the land in the area, he claimed 600 acres along the Rock River and settled in Fort Atkinson in 1838, becoming one of the most successful farmers in the area. Like many early settlers, Jones was very involved in community affairs, serving as a justice of the peace, postmaster, village president, and the first mayor of the city. It was his son, Milo II, who first began selling the now famous Jones Dairy Farm Sausages.

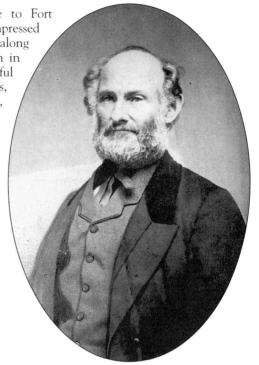

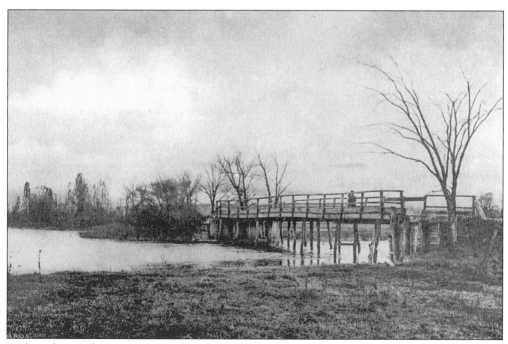

Built at the confluence of the Bark and Rock Rivers, the Bark River Bridge brought visitors into Fort Atkinson from the east. This picture dates from about the turn of the century.

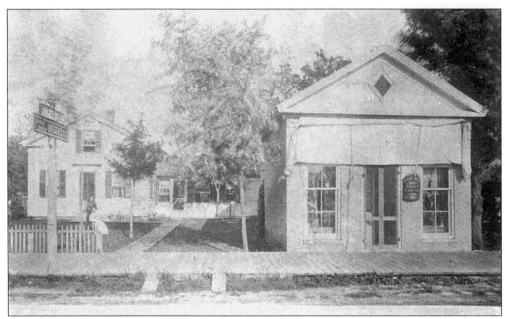

L.B. Caswell opened the first bank, called the Bank of Koshkonong, in Jefferson County in 1857. Its currency featured two Native Americans in a canoe gathering rice on Lake Koshkonong. When this picture was taken, the building was being used as a millinery store. Note the wooden sidewalks.

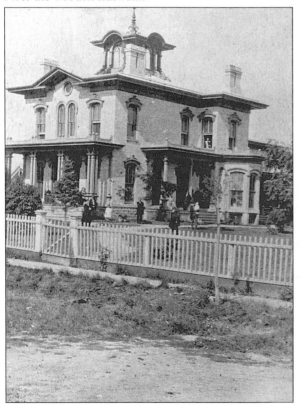

Lucien Bonapart Caswell was one of Fort Atkinson's most distinguished citizens. A lawyer, banker, and a U.S. congressman for 14 years, Caswell served the city in many ways, including an amazing 65 years on the school board! This house, designed in the Italianate style popular at the time, was built in 1873 and was a grand showplace with seven bedrooms and marble staircases. Unfortunately, the home was demolished in 1955 to make way for the present Catholic church.

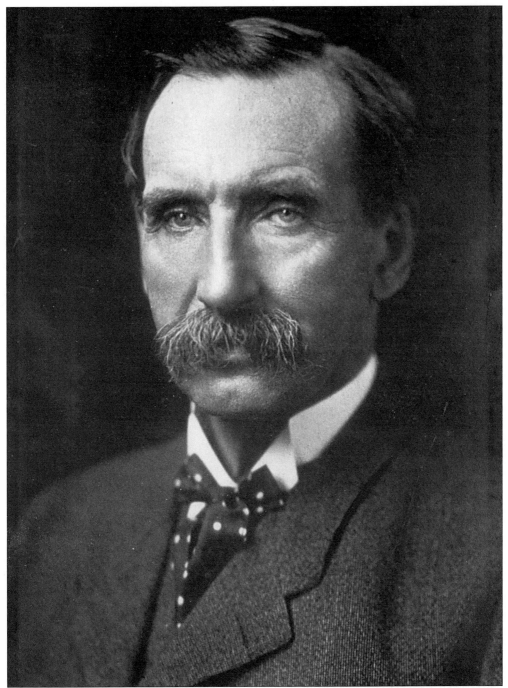

William Dempster Hoard (1836-1918) was born in New York and came to Wisconsin in 1857. After trying his hand at a number of careers, Hoard settled down to begin a newspaper, the *Jefferson County Union*. He went on to have a distinguished career founding the ongoing *Hoard's Dairyman* magazine in 1885 and serving as a progressive governor of Wisconsin from 1888 to 1890. Throughout his life, W.D. Hoard was a tireless champion and promoter of the dairy industry.

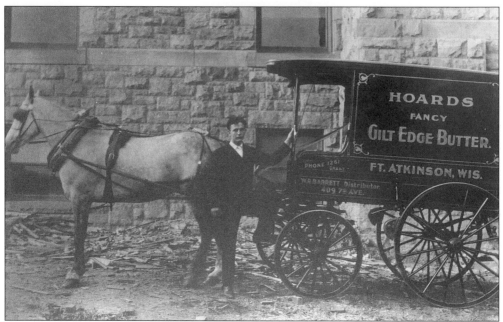

Arthur Hoard began Hoard's Creamery in 1886. His butter captured the Gold Medal at the 1893 World's Fair in Chicago. By 1900, the Creamery produced over 600,000 pounds of butter, shipped weekly to more than 7,000 families and 100 hotels in Chicago, St. Louis, and Pittsburgh.

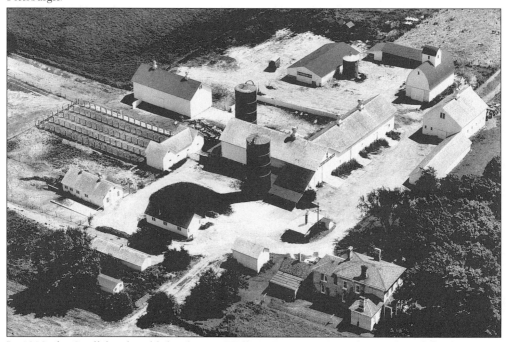

In 1899, the Snell family sold this farm to William Dempster Hoard. Hoard used the farm as an experimental laboratory where he could implement all the latest dairy ideas and new technologies advocated by his *Hoard's Dairyman* magazine. One hundred years later, it is still going strong as a working dairy farm.

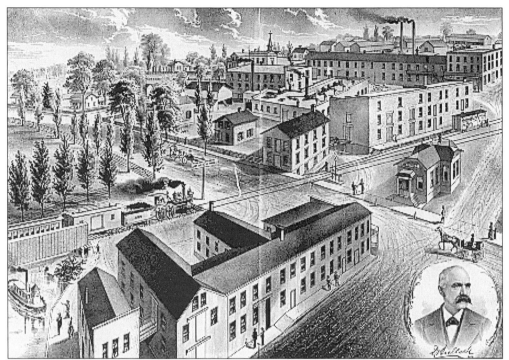

Founded in 1865, the Northwestern Furniture Company produced a wide variety of quality furniture and wagons. It was one of the largest furniture plants in the state, employing 250 people by 1897. After a series of business reverses, the company went bankrupt in 1923. The small office building in the right center of the picture is the only part of the complex that is still standing.

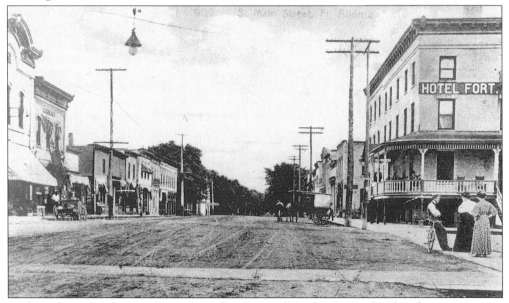

Looking down South Main Street from the corner of South Main and Milwaukee, one can see the Green Mountain House, which has now become the Hotel Fort. Note the wooden sidewalks and crosswalk.

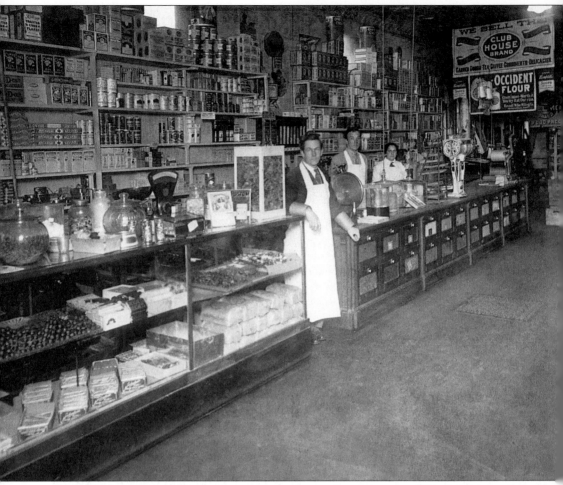

W.B. Black purchased his grocery store on the southeast corner of South Main and South Water Street in 1911. In addition to his cash and carry plan, Black charged 5 cents for every delivery and 1 cent on the dollar, or a fraction thereof, for credit. This picture was taken about 1915.

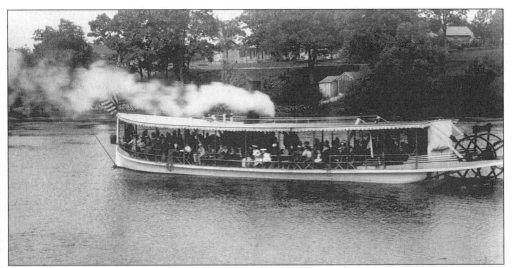

The most famous of all the Rock River-Lake Koshkonong boats was the *Uncle Sam*. It was built in 1898 for Arthur Hoard. The paddler, capable of handling 175 passengers, ran all summer between downtown Fort Atkinson and Hoard's Hotel on Lake Koshkonong (now the site of the Koshkonong Mounds Country Club). A round trip ticket cost .25 cents.

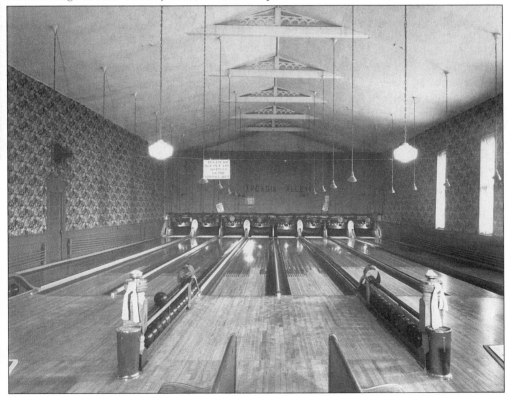

The Arcadia Bowling Alley building on East Milwaukee Avenue originally housed all the city offices, including the police and fire departments. In 1910, the building was sold to William Lloyd, who transformed it into the popular Lyric Theater. It was subsequently sold to the Herro family, who opened the Arcadia Bowling Alley.

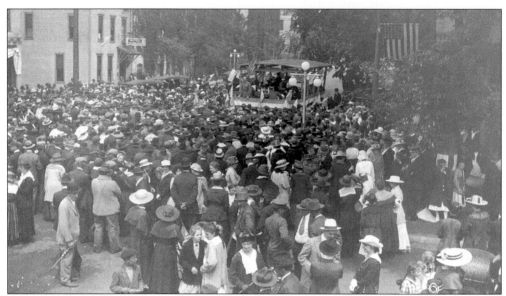

Large crowds gathered around the train depot on a number of occasions throughout 1919 to welcome home soldiers returning from World War I. It is interesting to note that this was certainly a hat-wearing era as almost everyone, men and women, are wearing hats.

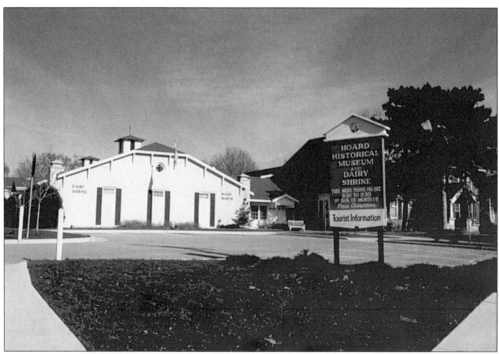

Located in an 1864 historic house, the Hoard Historical Museum boasts 16 exhibit rooms, ranging from period rooms to modern exhibits. The National Dairy Shrine Visitor's Center was constructed adjacent to the Hoard Museum and features an extensive display of dairy artifacts.

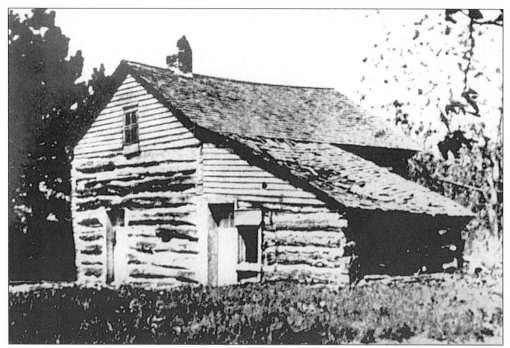

This cabin, located in the town of Sumner, was the home of Thure Kumlien, famed Norwegian naturalist. He kept an extensive diary of his life here in Jefferson County, and many of his specimens are on display in the Hoard Historical Museum.

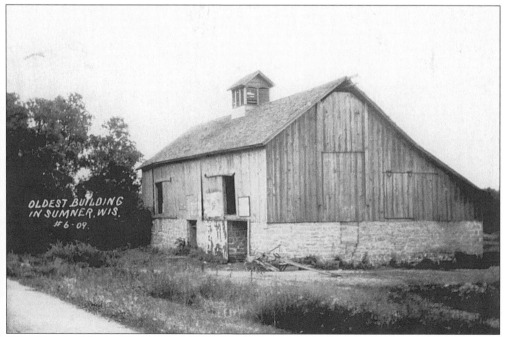

The oldest building in Sumner was this barn, built in the 1840s. It is no longer standing.

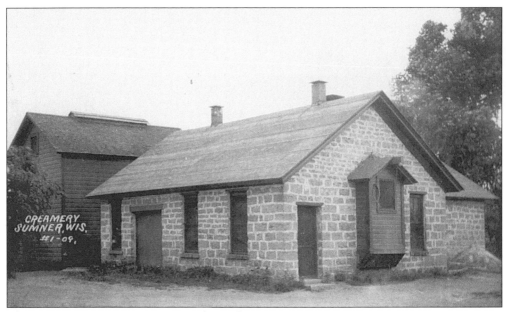

The Sumner creamery was a major industry for many years.

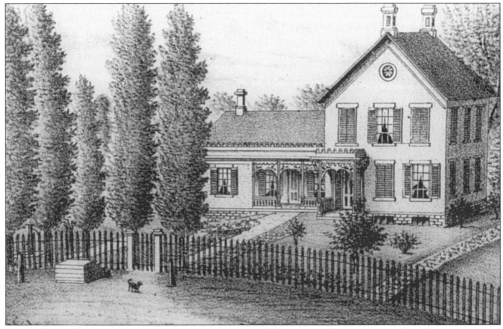

The John Whittet home in Sumner is pictured here. In the summer of 1850, James and Margaret, along with their two sons, James D. and John, came to Wisconsin from Scotland and settled in Sumner Township. The senior Whittet, soon after, bought a 120-acre farm; he died in 1871. John helped his father and then bought his own farm in Sumner.

Five
JEFFERSON

The city of Jefferson, situated in the center of the county, serves as the county seat. The Jefferson County Courthouse is located here, the present building having been erected in the late 1960s. The history of the city, however, goes back to the very beginnings of the county.

The settlement of the city began in 1836, when Rodney Currier and Daniel Lansing built a log hut at the mouth of the Crawfish and Rock Rivers. They were soon followed by Robert Masters and his family and others, and the town began. In October 1837, the first frame house was erected on the site now occupied by Miss Kitty's, a popular restaurant. This building was not only a home, but it also served as a hotel, a tavern, a courthouse and a general store.

By 1845, the population was between 75 or 80 people. Businesses at this time included a blacksmith shop, a gun smith shop, county buildings, and a school. The city continued to grow, and as the years passed, more services for the betterment of the residents were provided, including police and fire protection, a library, and fair grounds.

Jefferson is known for its outstanding county fair, which was been held annually since 1853. Each year hundreds of local farmers use the fair to showcase their produce and livestock, and through the years the Jefferson County Fair has become one of the best county fairs in the state.

Today, Jefferson is a thriving, modern city, with varied industry. It is home to the annual Gemutlichkeit Days, a festival that showcases the city's German heritage, as well as the Council for the Performing Arts. To say that Jefferson is the "biggest little town you'll ever love" is an understatement.

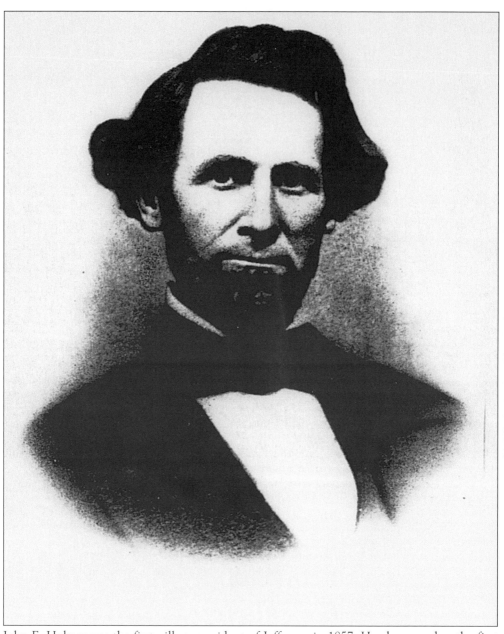

John E. Holmes was the first village president of Jefferson in 1857. He also served as the first lieutenant governor of the State of Wisconsin from 1840 to 1850. He is buried in Greenwood Cemetery in Jefferson, and his final resting place is listed on the city's historic register.

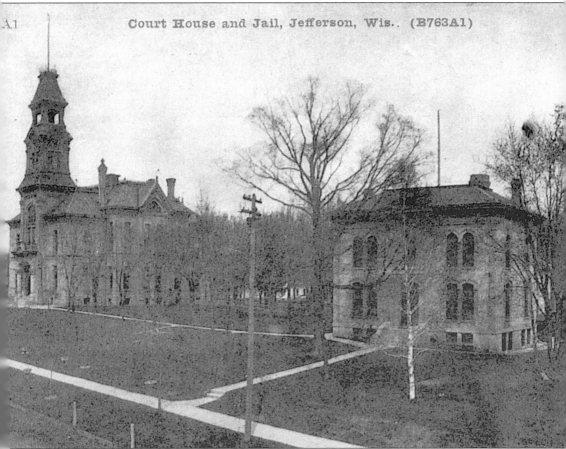

The old courthouse and county jail were built in the 1880s at a cost of $36,000. These buildings served the county until the present courthouse was built in the late 1960s.

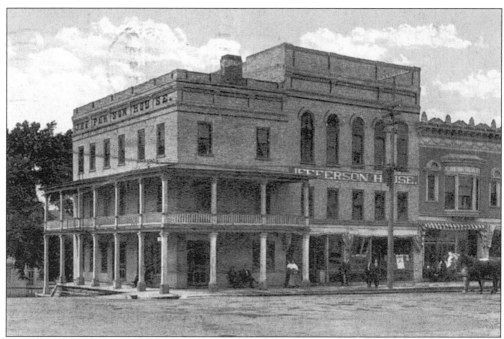

The Jefferson House is one of the oldest remaining buildings. The oldest part of the building was brought on a barge down the river from the town of Hebron. This has been at various times a courthouse, a hotel, an eatery, and a tavern. Presently, it is a restaurant called Miss Kitty's Jefferson House.

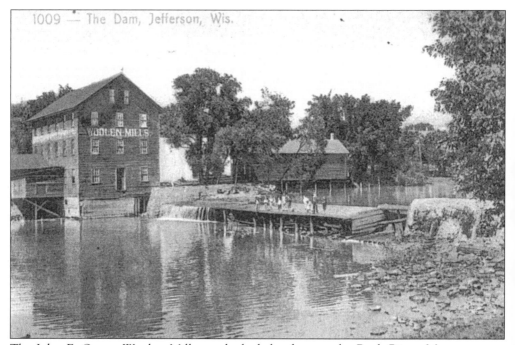

The John E. Owens Woolen Mills overlooked the dam on the Rock River. Many a young fisherman caught "a big one" here.

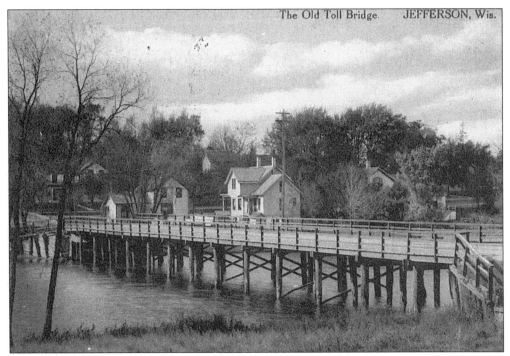

The old wooden toll bridge on North Street crossing the Rock River is a throwback to the early days of the county. The original toll was a penny. This bridge has been preserved as a footbridge.

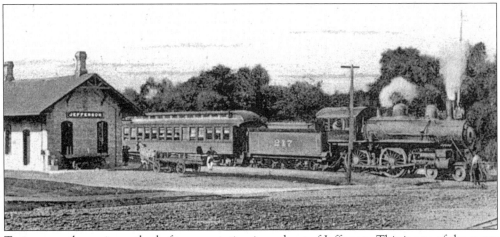

Trains were the main method of transportation in and out of Jefferson. This is one of the many stations that presidential candidates, such as Teddy Roosevelt, stopped at during whistle-stop campaigns.

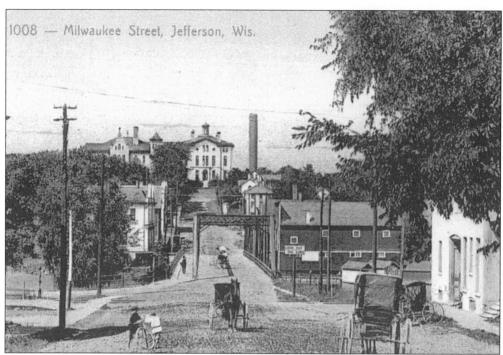

Many a student crossed the Rock River on the old Milwaukee Street bridge to attend the high school on the hill.

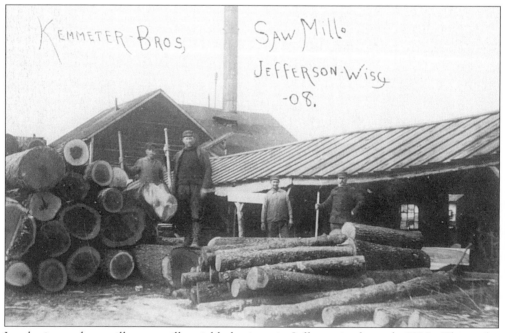

Lumbering and sawmills were still a viable business in Jefferson in the early 1900s. This is the Kemmeter Brothers Saw Mill in 1908.

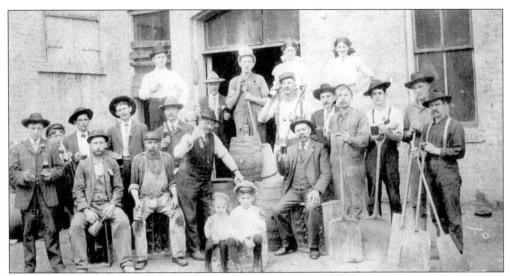

The workers and family of the R. Heger Brewery, one of five breweries in Jefferson, pose for this picture. From left to right are (front row) Jacob Grill, Henry Kaukaskie, Fred Zobel, John Bauer Sr. (brew master), August Bergholtz, and John Geyer; (middle row) Jake Neis, Reed Heger, Frank Aumann, Henry Vogel, George Welter, Charles Roessler, Charles Goetz, Reuben Heger, and Fred Rockstroh; (back row) Joe Hauer, Henry Perkins, Bill Heiden, Miranda Heger, and Carrie Heger. On the beer cases are Ivo Heger (left) and Cyril Heger (right).

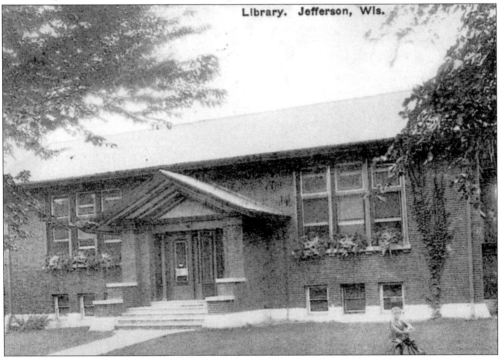

The Carnegie Building, which was the old public library, is now on the city's historic register, as well as the National Register. It is one of the few Prairie styles of architecture still in its original form in Jefferson. Today, this building houses the Jefferson Historical Society. A new library was built in the 1980s.

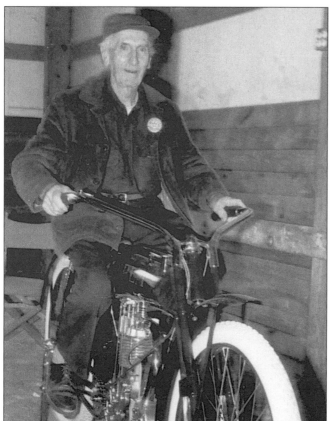

Ivo Heger, a descendant of Rudolph Heger, the brewer, sits on a Jefferson Motorcycle, built in Jefferson between 1911 to 1914. Ivo was a shareholder in the motorcycle company. This cycle was also known as the Jefferson and the Waverly.

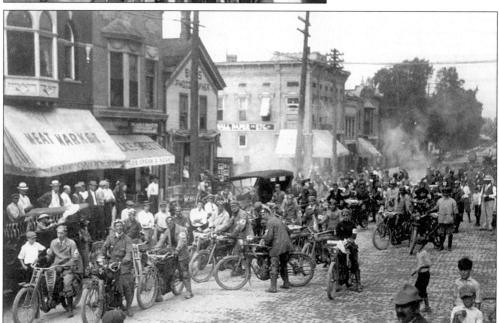

This motorcycle race in Jefferson was photographed c. 1912. Many of the cycles in this race were made in Jefferson.

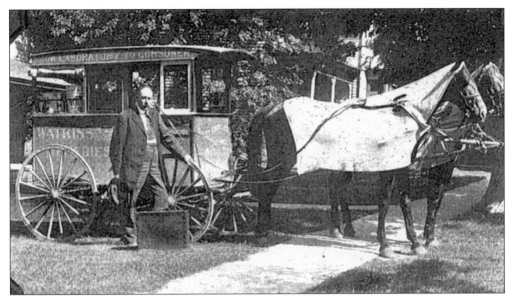

Floyd Fisher was the founder of the Bon Ton Bakery. Today, his great-grandson carries on the business. Note that at this time Fisher was still using a horse and wagon in his business.

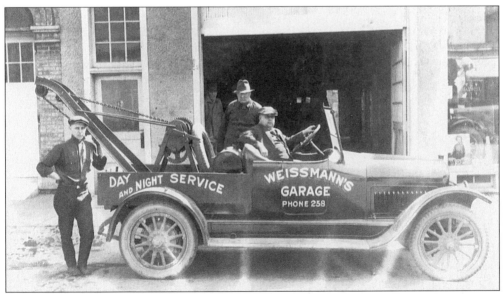

As automobiles became more common place, garages began to open up. One such garage was Weissmann's on East Milwaukee Street. Owner George Weissmann is shown seated in the wrecker and his son, Florian, is by the hoist. John Gering and Lambert Reuth look on. The Weissmann family also owned a bakery and a beauty shop on Milwaukee Street.

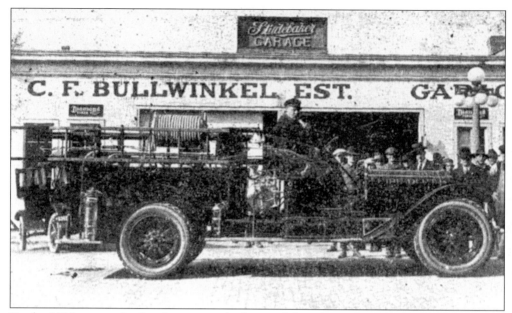

By the 1910s, even the fire department had moved from horse-drawn vehicles to motorized ones. This picture shows the old fire truck in front of the C.F. Bullwinkel Garage on East Milwaukee Street.

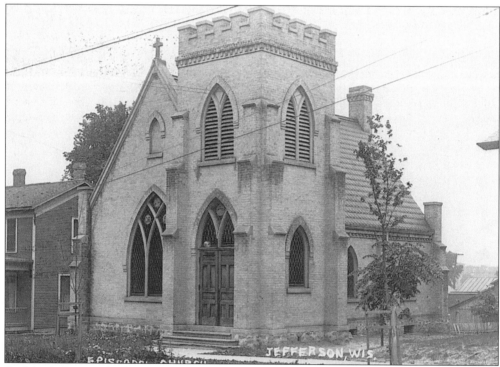

St. Mary's Episcopal Church was at one time located on South Main Street. This building is now the home of the Fidelity Land Title Ltd. office.

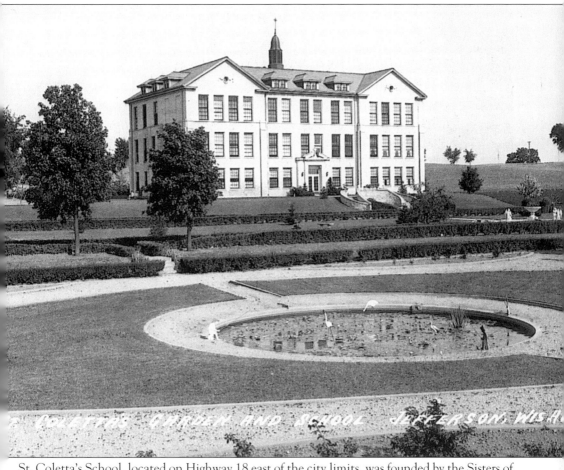

St. Coletta's School, located on Highway 18 east of the city limits, was founded by the Sisters of Saint Francis Assisi on September 5, 1904. The facility was founded with the purpose of training mentally retarded children. It has become a nationally known school for the training of those who wish to work with developmentally challenged children and adults.

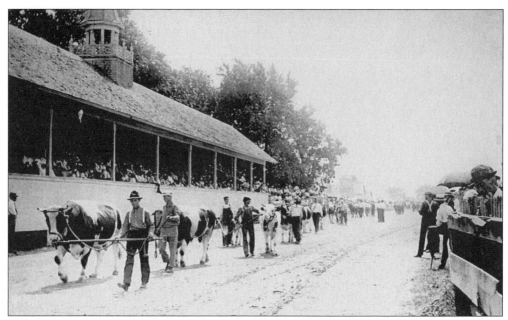

Holsteins are shown here on parade at the Jefferson County Fair about 1910. Started in 1853, the Jefferson County Fair has grown to be one of the better fairs in the state.

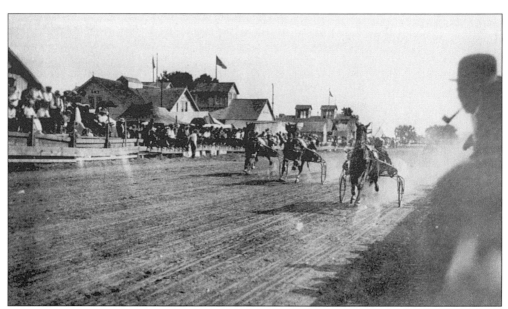

A trotting race at the fair, c. 1910, is pictured here. Originally, the fair was held in various places throughout the county, but since 1866 it has always been held at Jefferson.

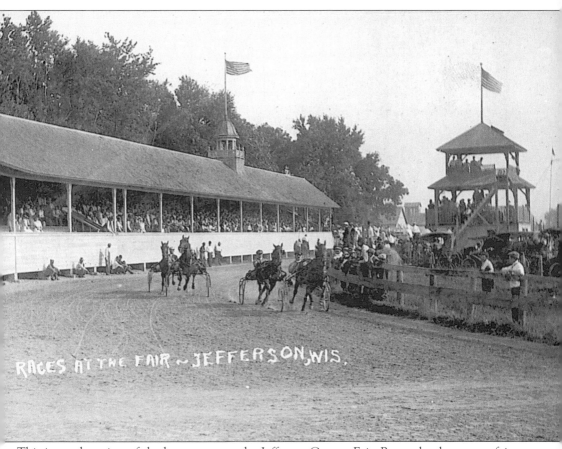

This is another view of the horse races at the Jefferson County Fair. Recently, the county fair grounds underwent extensive remodeling, thus making it a more comfortable and accessible place to hold the annual event.

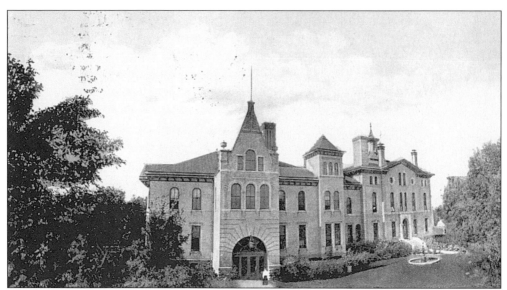
The old high school in Jefferson was originally known as the Jefferson Liberal Institute and opened its doors in 1866. It was destroyed by fire in 1924.

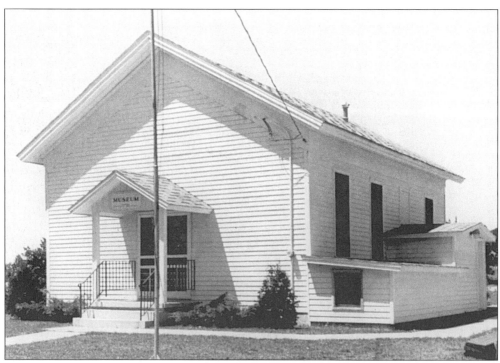
The City of Jefferson has two museums, the Bakertown School Museum and the Jefferson Historical Society. The Bakertown School houses artifacts from early days in the county and early school days, while the Jefferson Historical Society, which meets in the old Carnegie Library building on Main Street, is home to the archives of the historical society.

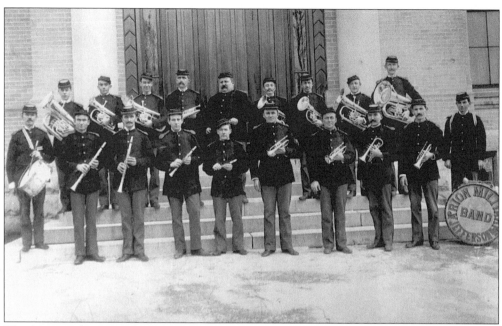

The Arion Military Band was one of many early musical groups in Jefferson.

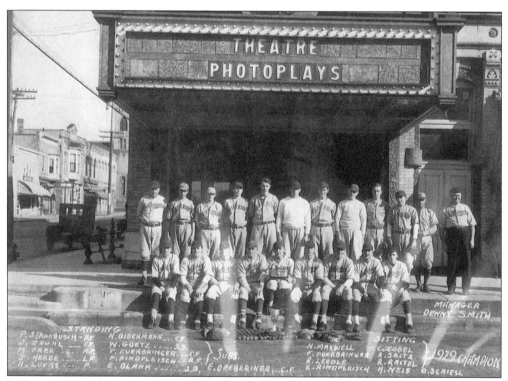

Jefferson's 1929 championship baseball team stands in front of the Opera House Theater, now the site of the Farmers and Merchants Bank.

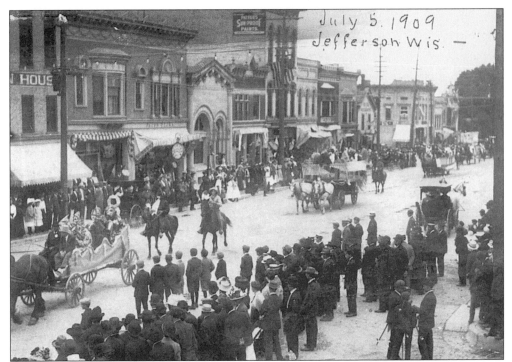

A Fourth of July celebration down the red brick Main Street was the social gathering of the summer. Portions of this red brick road still exist on Gardner Street, part of the historic district of Jefferson.

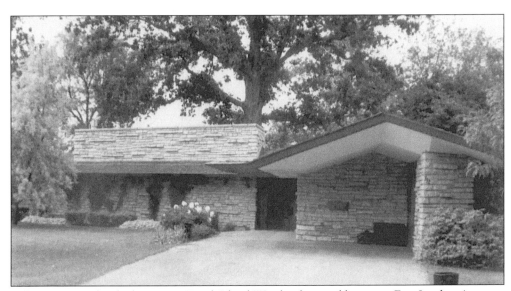

Jefferson is proud to be home to a Frank Lloyd Wright-designed home on East Linden Avenue. This is a front view of the home, which was built in 1950.

Six
Johnson Creek

The present village of Johnson Creek had its inception in 1838, when Timothy Johnson and Charles Goodhue made a claim upon land where the main part of the village is now located. They built a cabin on ground over which the Northwestern Railroad now runs. A dam and a sawmill were also constructed by the same men.

Progress was slow, but by 1879, there were two stores, two churches, three saloons, two blacksmith shops, two wagon shops, two shoe shops, one implement dealer, one cheese factory, one commission warehouse, one feed mill, two hotels, one lumber yard, a district schoolhouse, and a drug store.

Prominent members of the community included members of the Mansfield family. George C. Mansfield was a pioneer in the butter, milk, and egg trade. He started a cheese factory and later became the state's leading butter producer. In 1888, he started the Mansfield Bank, a commercial system necessary to the success of any village.

The railroad arrived in Johnson Creek in 1859 and, with it, the first railroad tragedy. On November 1, 1859, a train traveling 15 miles an hour en route from Chicago struck a large ox. The train was derailed and the cars sent into a marshy area. Fourteen people were killed in the accident and at least 30 were injured.

Johnson Creek is now known as "The Crossroads With A Future." Many new homes and apartments are being built. The village has its own medical clinic, library, veterinary service, and smaller businesses. Present industries include Hi-Life Rubber, Bobcat, Master Mold, Polydyne, Saelens Corporation, and the Equity Livestock Auction. The village has a high school, built in 1958, and an elementary school, built in 1964. Enrollment in these schools numbers 600.

The village keeps growing with the addition of its first movie theater and fast food restaurant, and the Johnson Creek Outlet Mall, which opened in 1998.

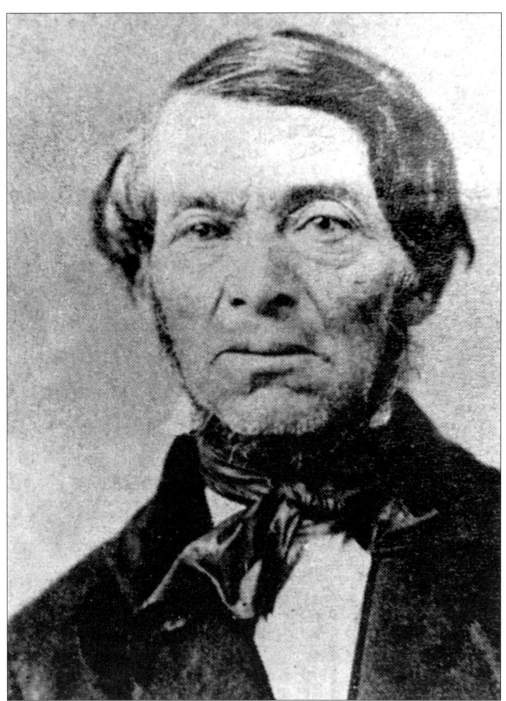

The founder of Johnson Creek was Timothy Johnson (1792–1871), who came to this place in 1838. He had previously held claims in Jefferson, Aztalan, and nearby Watertown, where he made his home for most of his life and is buried. Johnson and partner Charles Goodhue built a dam and a sawmill on the site of the present village and were the first settlers. The village is named for Johnson.

George C. Mansfield was an early businessman and manufacturer. He became the state's leading producer of butter and also founded the Mansfield Bank in 1888.

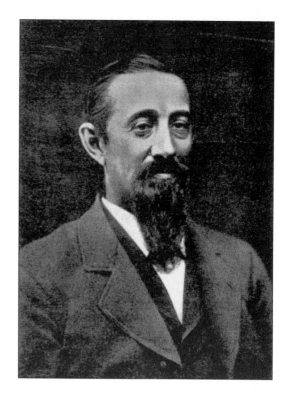

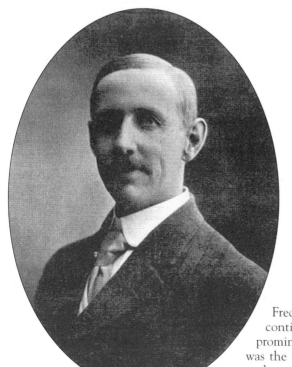

Fred C. Mansfield, the son of George C., continued the family tradition and became a prominent businessman in Johnson Creek. He was the first village president and, for 30 years, served on the school board. He was active in all civic affairs of the village.

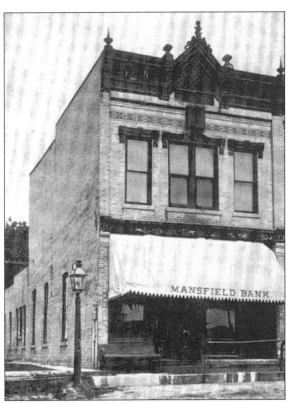

The Mansfield Bank was founded by George C. Mansfield in 1888.

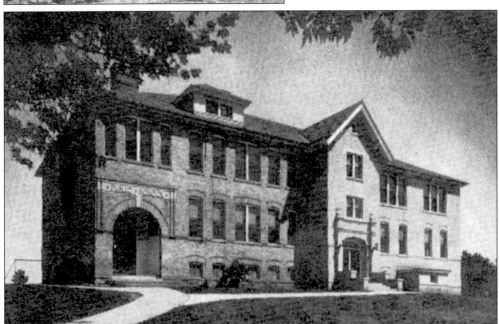

The Johnson Creek High School served students until the 1950s, when the present high school was built. An addition was built in 1925 through the generous donation of Fred C. Mansfield. This school also served the Farmington Township, in which the village of Johnson Creek is located.

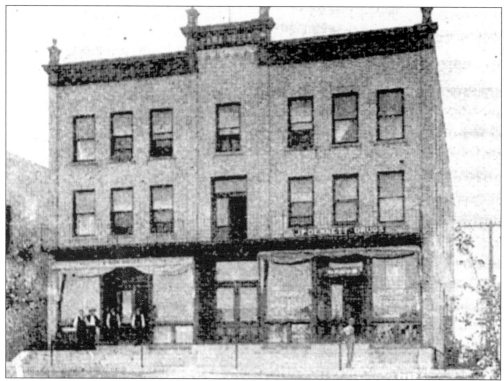

The Park Hotel was a popular gathering place in the early days of Johnson Creek. The building contained 24 sleeping rooms, a bar room, a barber shop, an office, a dining room, and a bowling alley. The hotel was built in 1895. The Hofbrau Bar is now located in the building, and the upper quarters have been remodeled into apartments. For many years the hotel was also the location of The Music Box, a popular local tavern.

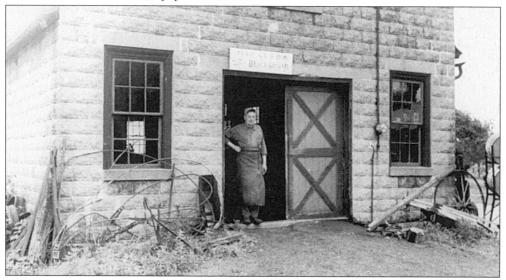

Otto Sukow's blacksmith shop was, for many years, a warm reminder of when everything was done by horses. Sukow ran the shop until the 1980s; it was a local landmark in the town of Farmington.

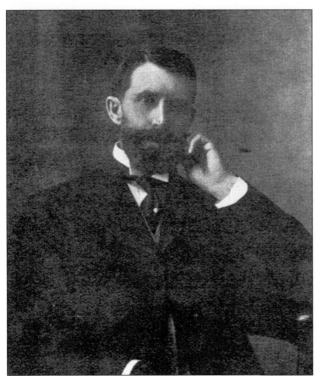

H.C. Christians established the butter and egg business in Johnson Creek in 1882. His firm was among the largest suppliers of butter in the state. His son, W.A. Christians, later organized a printing firm and the Rock River Telephone Company, furnishing the village with a modern telephone exchange and erecting rural lines in every direction.

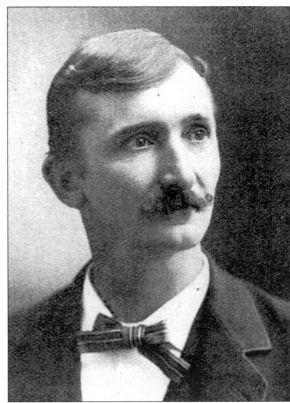

H.J. Grell was a another well-known businessman in Johnson Creek. He was also established in the butter and egg business and, in the late 1800s, served as president of the village.

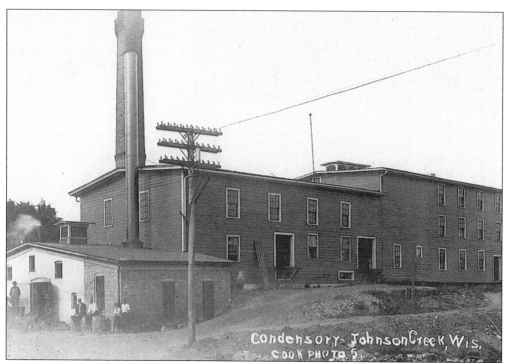

The milk condensory at Johnson Creek, pictured here in the early 1900s, was a very busy place. Today, Avon Hi-Life Inc. (formerly the Hi-Life Rubber Company) occupies this site.

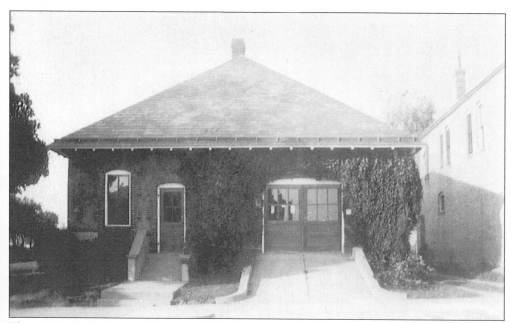

The original village hall, library, and fire department for Johnson Creek were located in this structure. Today, this is an office building.

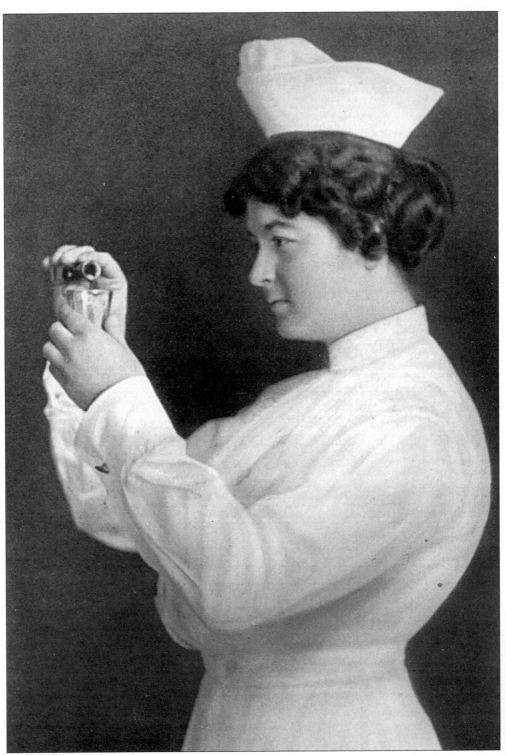
Hattie Raithel, a resident of Johnson Creek, was a nurse in World War I. She died overseas during the influenza epidemic of 1918.

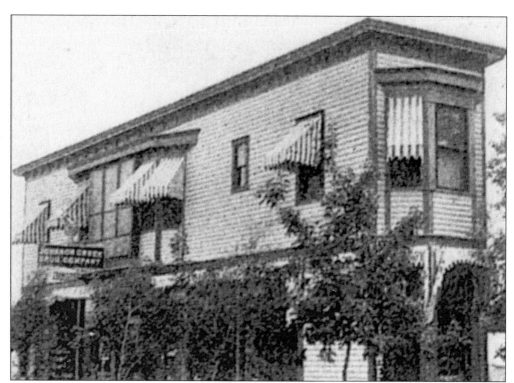

The Johnson Creek Drug Co. was founded in 1888 by J.P. Dennett and was incorporated in 1908. This building was later torn down, and today, the land upon which this building stood is part of Johnson Creek Park.

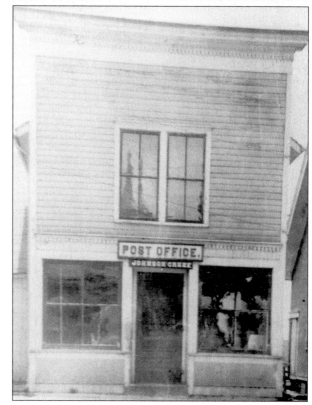

The Johnson Creek Post Office is pictured here in the early 1930s. Today, an office and an apartment are located in this building.

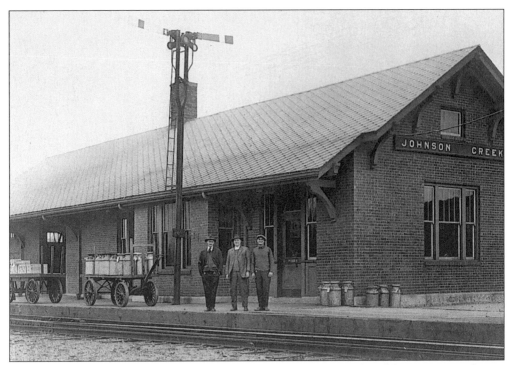

The Johnson Creek depot is seen here in the early 1900s. The railroad first came to Johnson Creek in 1859. This depot was later razed, and the municipal building was built on this location. Standing out front, from left to right, are Erwin Zimmerman, Ernie Burleton, and Herbert Kiepert.

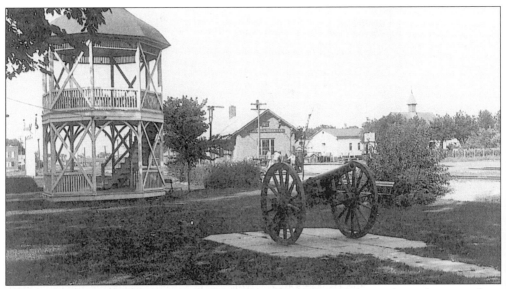

Taken in the early 1930s, this picture shows the village park with its gazebo and cannon from World War I. Note the depot in the background.

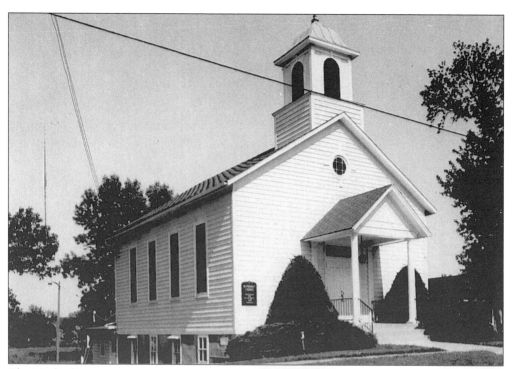

The Methodist congregation was organized in 1860, and the first church was erected in 1867 on land donated by Shep Griffin.

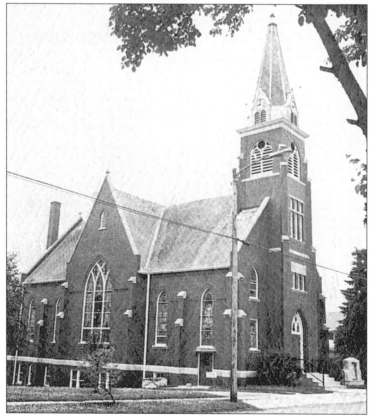

The St. John's Evangelical Lutheran congregation was founded in 1885. The present church was built in 1910 and was dedicated in 1911. Among the unusual features of this church is its "player-piano" organ.

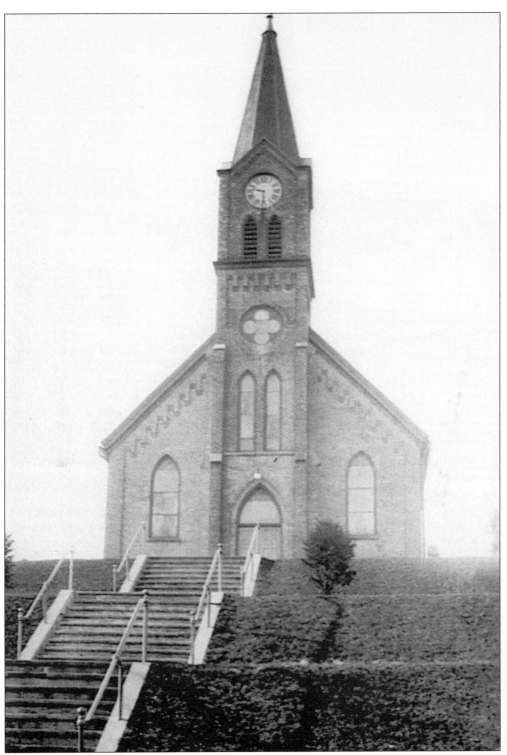

St. Mary Magdalene Catholic Church, shown here in the early 1900s, was organized in 1906. The cornerstone was laid in 1907, the year the church was built.

Seven
PALMYRA

The first settler to locate in what later the became the village of Palmyra was Cyrus Horton of Vermont. He built the first frame house in 1839. Shortly thereafter, Abram Brink began construction of the first dam and mill on the Scuppernong River. David and Samuel Powers soon arrived, and they bought the mill and began to deal in land. They commissioned John Fish to plat out the village and successfully lobbied to bring the railroad into the area in 1852. They are also credited with naming the town. Since the sandy areas between the springs reminded them of the Syrian Palmyra of Biblical times, they chose the name accordingly. The village was incorporated in 1874.

One of the landmarks that put Palmyra's name on everyone's lips in the latter half of the 19th century was the discovery of the Palmyra Springs. In 1871, Victor Loewe was clearing land on his farm when one of his workers unearthed a spring. As time went on, his farm hands claimed that drinking that spring water cured them of all kinds of pains and ailments. More springs were discovered in the immediate vicinity, each one having a different mineral content. Ira Bidwell, a wealthy man from St. Paul, was "taking the waters" at a spa in Waukesha when he heard about the Palmyra springs. He had the water tested and, after getting the results, began to buy up the land that contained some of the springs. Palmyra became a boom town.

Bidwell opened the Bidwell House, which later became the Spring Lake Hotel, and ran it successfully for many years. By the beginning of the 20th century, interest in mineral springs began to die out, and the hotel closed. The hotel was torn down many years later.

Other prominent businessmen included Otto Scherer, who had a unique mall-like office building, which housed a business office, an auto dealership and repair, a movie theater, a gymnasium, and a dance hall.

Today, Palmyra has five restaurants, a hardware store, gift shops, insurance offices, and other stores. In the summer, visitors come to Palmyra to ride their horses, swim, use the airport, and to see the historic Carlin House Museum. In the winter, they come for the snowmobiling and cross-country skiing. All in all, Palmyra is a pleasant place to live.

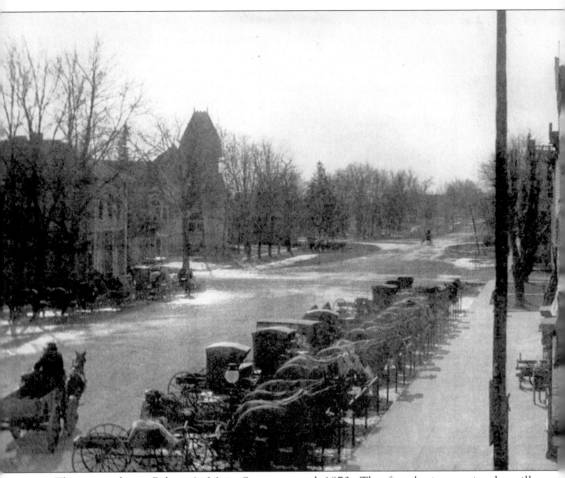
This view shows Palmyra's Main Street around 1870. The first businesses in the village appeared in the 1840s, and it wasn't too long before most of the needs of the area folks could be met by the stores of Main Street.

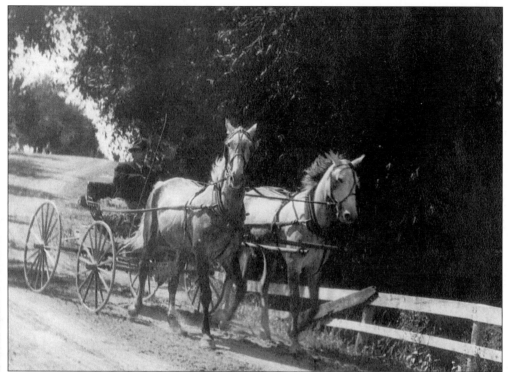

This is Christie Carlin and his fast team of horses going down the hill from downtown Palmyra to the Bidwell House, a spa and sanitarium. Mr. Carlin was the president of the Bank of Palmyra, and at one time, he owned the Bidwell House property. He sold it in 1922 to the National Association of Drug Clerks to make a home for retired druggists.

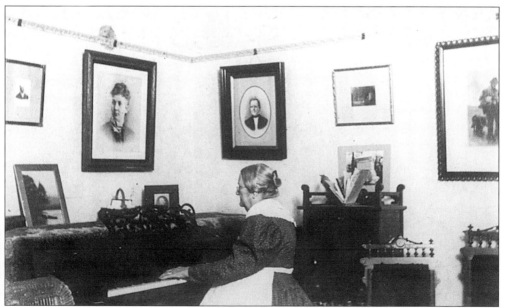

Mrs. William Carlin, the former Emma Hinton, wife of a prominent early settler, was the state's first piano teacher.

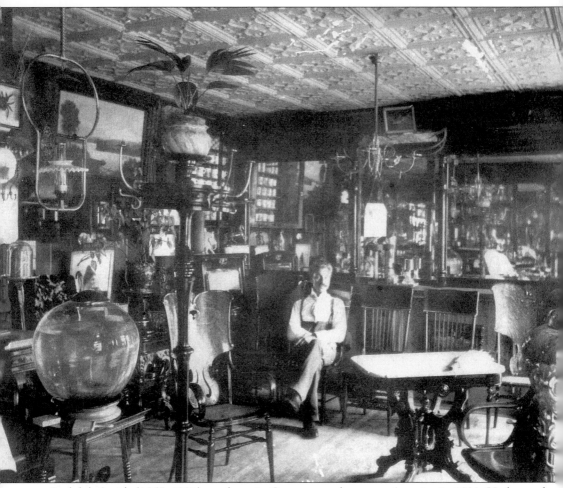

Rudolph Smith (1857–1931) was born in Germany and came to America in 1921. He learned the barber trade in Chicago, where he met his wife, Sophia Buchs, a native of Palmyra. They came to Palmyra, and he opened a shop called "the most beautiful barbershop in the world." Smith collected mounted birds and animals, rare shells and antiques, and made beautiful furniture.

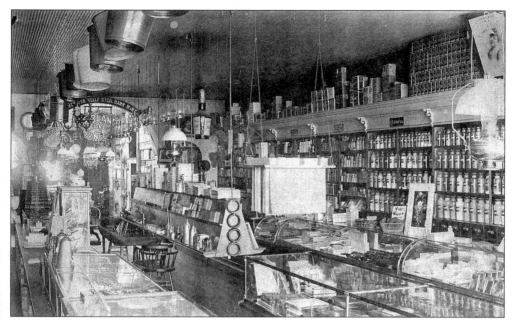

The interior of the Washburn drug store on Palmyra's Main Street is pictured here around 1880. The store first opened in 1876.

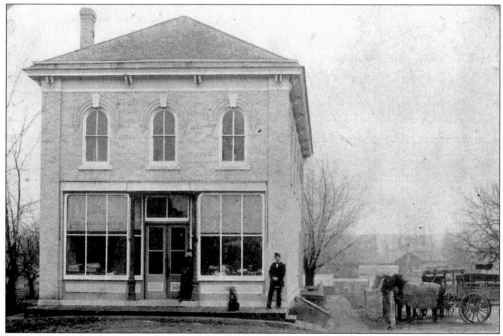

Mary and Erric Errickson are standing in front of the store they built in 1869 on Palmyra's Main Street. Mary was a professional milliner, and at first, the shop was a millinery store. Later, it became a dry goods store until it burned to the ground.

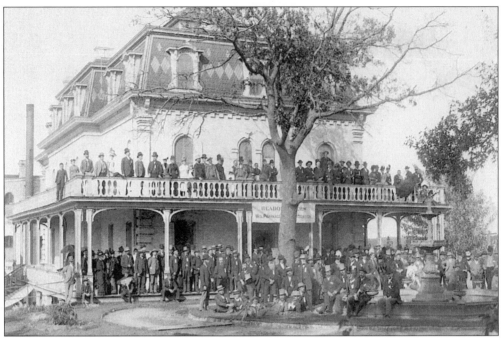

Palmyra's fling with fame was the result of the discovery of mineral springs in the area and the belief in their curative powers. The Bidwell House, shown here, was built in 1878 and had 152 rooms. In 1883, it was renamed the Palmyra Spring Sanitarium, and by 1887, it was known as the Spring Lake Hotel. In 1904, the hotel was used as a sanitarium for the care of mental patients. It passed through several different owners until being torn down in 1950.

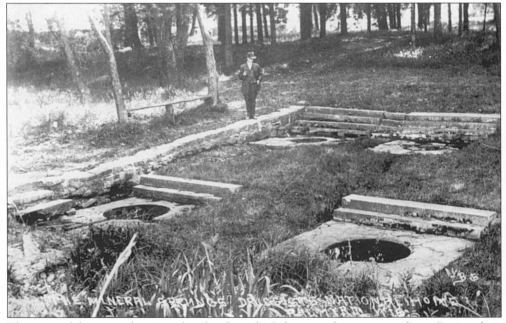

The ruins of the mineral springs that first brought Palmyra to fame are seen here. During their heyday, the springs were visited daily, and the nearby Bidwell House was a social center and spa for people from all over the country.

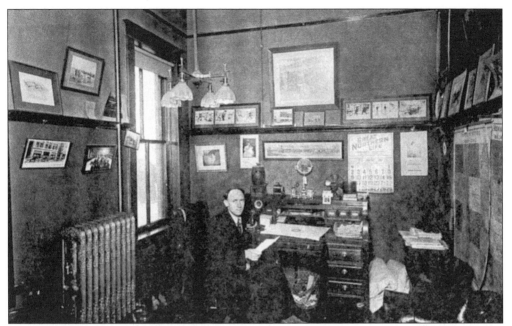

Otto E. Scherer (1872–1921) sold more Buicks than any other dealer in Wisconsin in the early part of this century. He bought a number of buildings in Palmyra, fixed them up, put his name on them, and sold them. An excellent salesman, he received an award in 1910 as the champion lightning rod salesman in the state and also won a prize for selling the most mowers, binders, and huskers for the International Harvester Co.

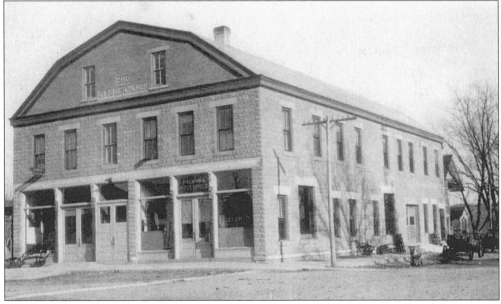

This was Otto Scherer's Buick Dealership and Opera House on Main and Third Streets in Palmyra. After the Errickson store burned, Scherer built this structure. The basement was a garage for repairing buggies and cars, the main floor contained his office and Buick sales area, and the upper floor had a dentist's office and a gymnasium-theater-ball room. It was the first building in Palmyra to be electrified and show motion pictures.

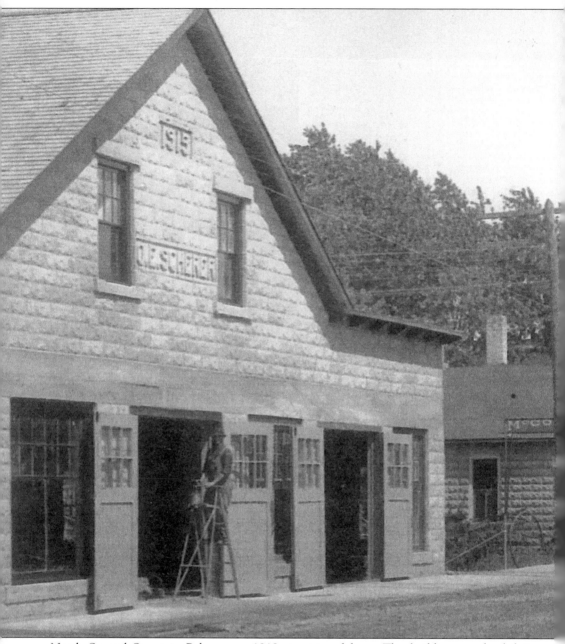

North Second Street in Palmyra, c. 1919, is pictured here. The building on the left is a car dealership, probably Ford. The middle building is a blacksmith shop with a buggy in front. At the corner of the street is a Model T coupe (first seen in 1908). Attached to the back of

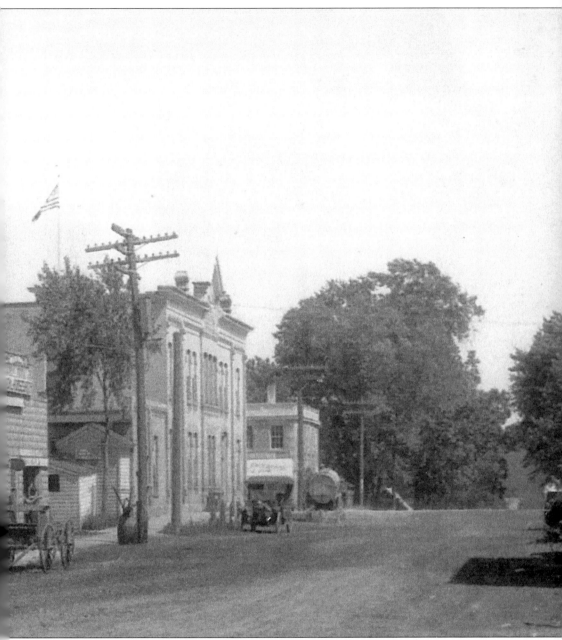

the Tisch House Hotel is an icehouse, but the electric pole signals that the end of the ice house is near.

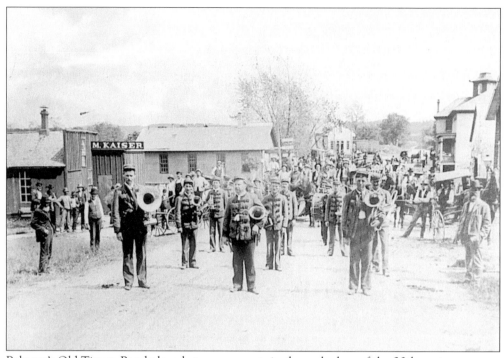
Palmyra's Old Timers Band played at many events in the early days of the 20th century.

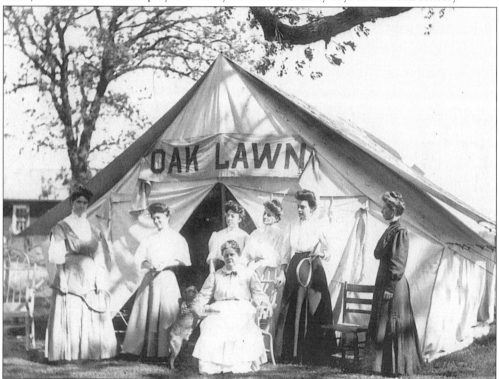
The Palmyra Oak Lawn Tennis Club is seen here around 1905. Tennis proved to be a popular sport with the ladies in the early days.

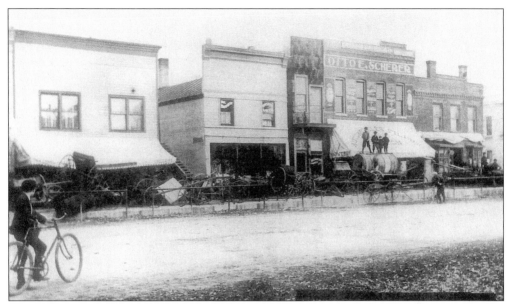

This Halloween prank of 1909 involved placing farm machinery on the Main Street sidewalk.

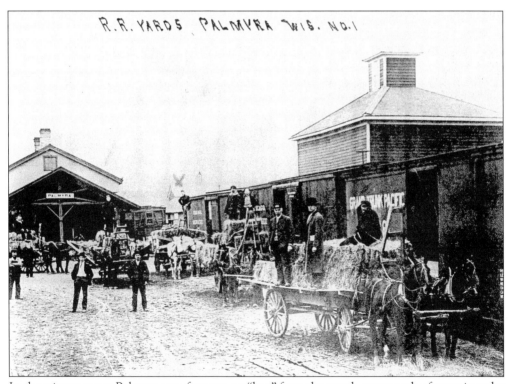

In the winter, many Palmyra-area farmers cut "hay" from the marsh grass north of town in order to feed livestock when the summer feed was used up, even though the hay had no nutritional value. In this picture, the hay is being shipped to Chicago to be used as packing for goods to be shipped. The marsh was a popular bird hunting area until the 1950s, when it was drained and cultivated for vegetable farming.

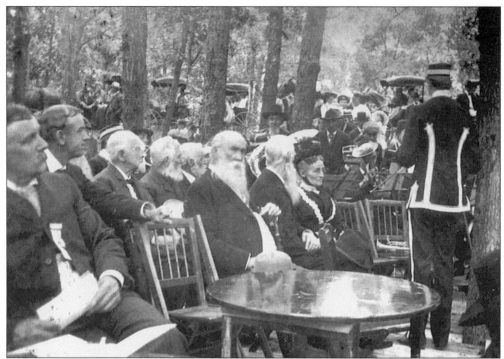

The first Old Settler's Reunion was held in 1885. It continues to this day as an annual event honoring citizens of outstanding value to the community.

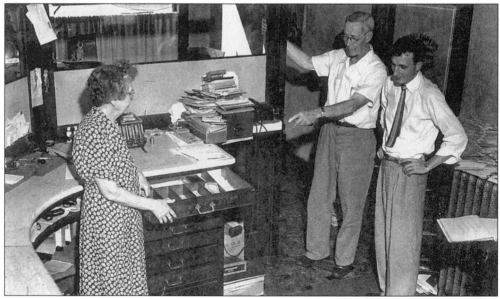

At 20 minutes past noon, on a Thursday in July 1952, a lone gunman entered the Palmyra State Bank and forced manager Bill Norris to give him $600 in small bills. The rest of the bank's employees were already out for lunch. The gunman made Bill lie on the floor, but as soon as he heard the robber's car leave, he leapt to his feet and gave chase with the bank's revolver. In spite of the police search, the robber was never found. Pictured here are bank clerk Ada Seamon, Bill Norris, and Dick Bischell, who would later become the bank manager.

Eight
ROME AND SULLIVAN

The township of Sullivan was originally part of the Bark River Woods, and by an act of the Territorial Legislature, it became Bark River Township. Cold Spring, Hebron, Sullivan, and Palmyra comprised this town until 1846 when the Territorial Legislature divided the township into individual groups. Cyrus Curtis was recorded as being the first permanent settler, having built a cabin here in 1837.

Settlements of the township included Rome. This tiny village was carved out of the Bark River Woods and through it runs the Bark River, which provided a lifeline for the early settlers, supporting early industries for growth and sustenance. The earliest settler was Peter Knockler and his family, who arrived in 1840 and built a log house.

In 1842, Myron Smith and S.D. Tenny arrived and built a sawmill. The mill burned, but another was soon built. At this time, settlers began arriving, among them the Seeley brothers, Ambrose, Davis, and Dempster. They purchased the mill and, with others, dug the mill race and built a sawmill and turning shop in 1852, part of which still stands.

On September 9, 1848, Ambrose Seely platted and recorded the Village of Rome, named for Rome, New York, where many of the settlers hailed from.

The Village of Sullivan, located in Town 6 North, was laid out in 1881 by Earl Newton and Enoch B. Fargo. The coming of the railroad promised great things for the little village, and before long, most of the business lots were sold and the village began to prosper. Sullivan is the only settlement in Town 6 North that has been incorporated into a village. This took place in 1915.

The wooden sidewalks, hitching posts, and old-time country stores are gone now, and those who remember the bustling activity of yesteryear are indeed fortunate. Truly, those were the "good old days."

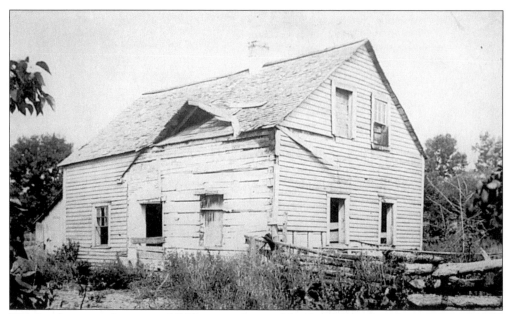
The first house in the town of Sullivan was erected by Cyrus Curtis in the summer of 1837. Curtis lived here alone from October 1838 until May 1839, when his family joined him. When this picture was taken, it was said to have been the oldest frame structure in Jefferson County.

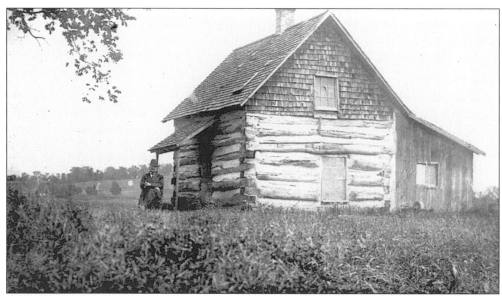
This is a picture of an early log cabin built by Eason Higbie at Heath's Mill, a little settlement within the township.

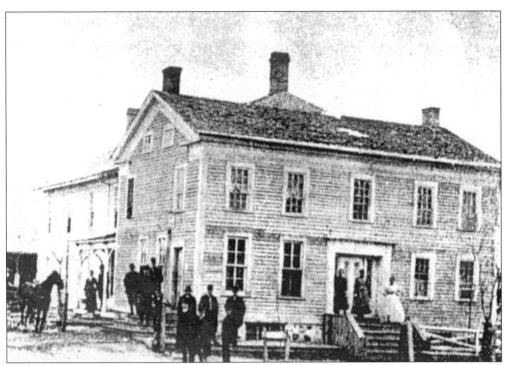

The "Live and Let Live" Hotel was built in the Town of Rome in 1848. This was a popular stopping spot for travelers.

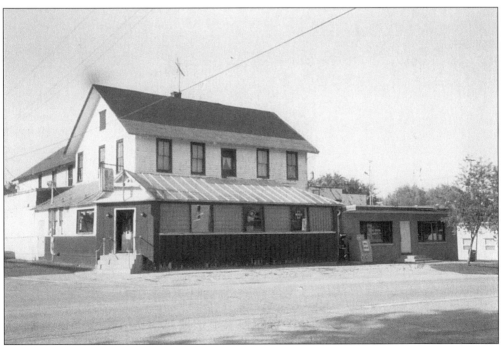

The "Live and Let Live" is now the Bark River Lanes, a bowling alley.

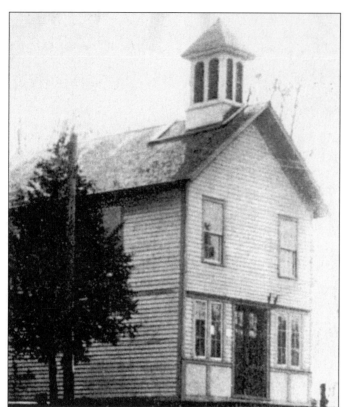

The old town hall was built about 1856 and has not changed significantly since that time.

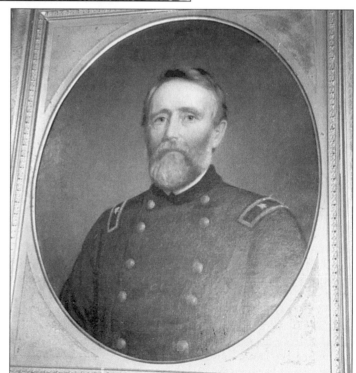

Colonel Henry Harnden was a resident of Rome, Wisconsin. He and Colonel Pritchard of Michigan are credited with the capture of Jefferson Davis during the Civil War.

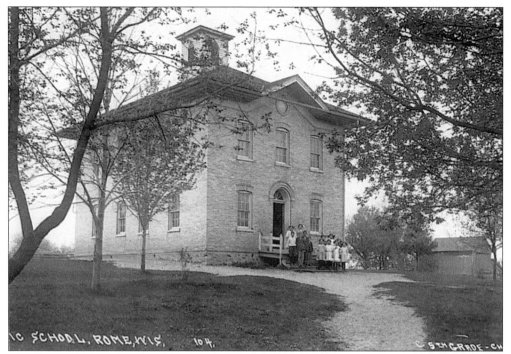

The Rome Public School was built in 1870. At that time, Rome boasted two public schools with belfries. Today, this is the home of the Rome-Sullivan Historical Society.

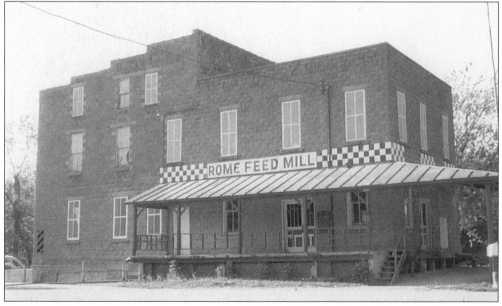

The Rome Feed Mill, shown here, is the last of a long line of mills that began in the township in the 1840s.

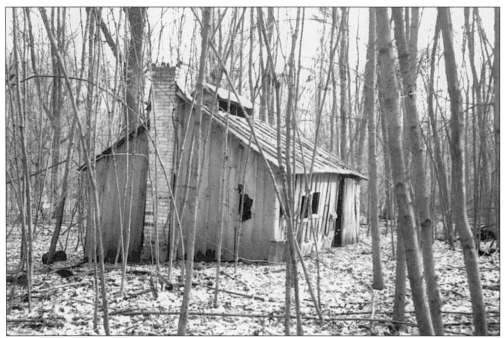

This was Sanses Mill in the 1890s. At the time this picture was taken, the mill was being used as a sugaring shack on the Debereiner Farm.

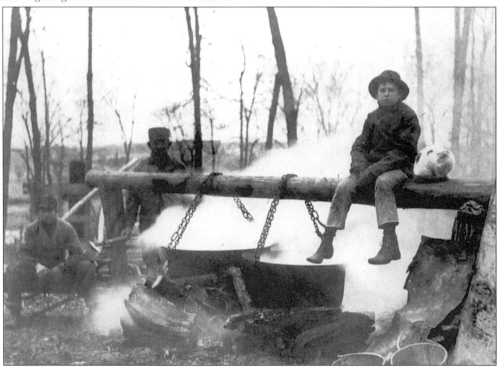

It's maple sugar time on the Joseph Boos farm. Making maple sugar was a favorite pastime, especially for the young people of the area. Pictured here, from left to right, are Joseph Boos, Tom Boos, and Guy Boos (on the log). This picture was taken on March 23, 1907.

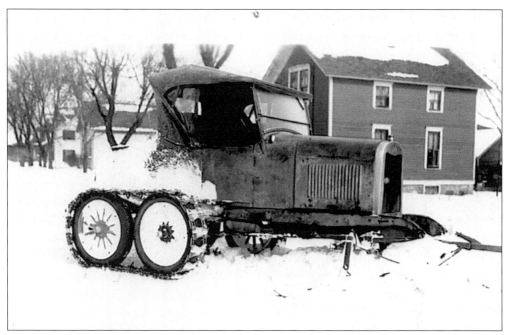

This snowmobile was invented by Sullivan mail carrier Walter Zahn in 1936. A similar vehicle was used at the South Pole.

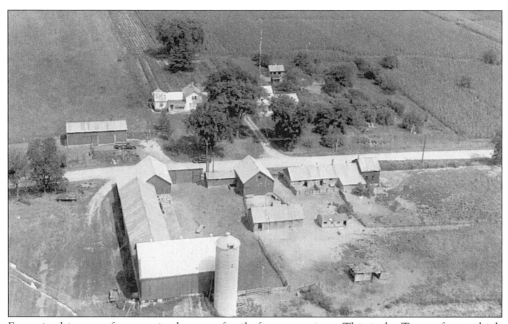

Farms in this area often stay in the same family for generations. This is the Turner farm, which has been owned by five generations of the same family since it was taken up from the government in 1843.

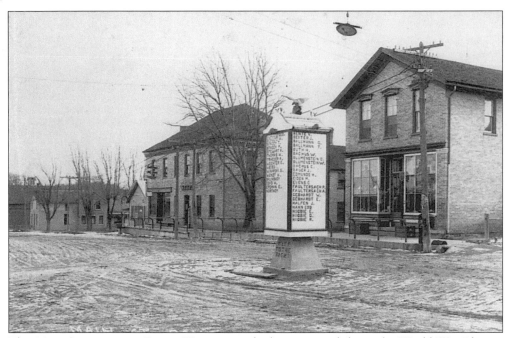
This Main Street view in Rome, Wisconsin is looking east and shows the World War I honor roll, Landgraf's Store, and the Ungermeyer building.

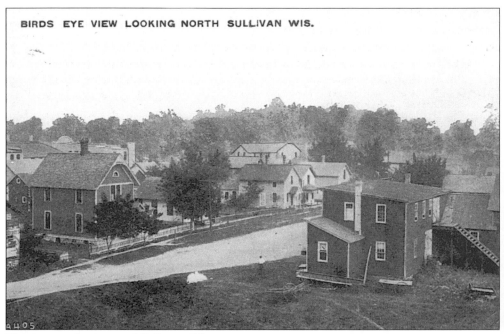
This is an early picture of Sullivan, Wisconsin.

Nine
WATERLOO

The City of Waterloo can trace its history back to 1842. In that year, Bradford L. Hill arrived in this area and purchased "two forties" in Section 5. Hill, a native of Vermont, settled here with his wife and four children, and other settlers soon followed. The Hill home was located on the eastern side of the Maunesha River.

The land now comprising the town and village of Waterloo was, prior to 1845, a part of the town of Aztalan. Waterloo became an independent town in 1846, and Abram Vanderpool was its first chairman. By 1848, Waterloo had 35 to 40 residents and 6 homes. By the 1850s, the population rose to about 200. Growth slackened during the Civil War but soon rose again in the years that followed, with a residential building boom in the 1890s.

Milling was a major industry here in the early days, and Waterloo was the leading grain market in the area. Other industries such as canning, shoe manufacturing, malting, popcorn growing, and cheese making once flourished here. Today, the city is the home of the Perry Printing Corporation and Trek Bicycles.

The railroad came through in 1859, making Waterloo a leading center for produce. A water works system was added in 1910 and an electric light plant in 1908. The first school opened in 1843. Today, the city is served by several parochial and public schools as well as several churches. Waterloo was granted its city status in 1962.

A small community, the citizens of Waterloo are proud of their roots. The Waterloo Area Historical Society has its headquarters in the old St. Joseph's Catholic Church. Their annual Fourth of July celebration is held in beautiful Fireman's Park, and each September, the whole city turns out for Weiner and Kraut Day.

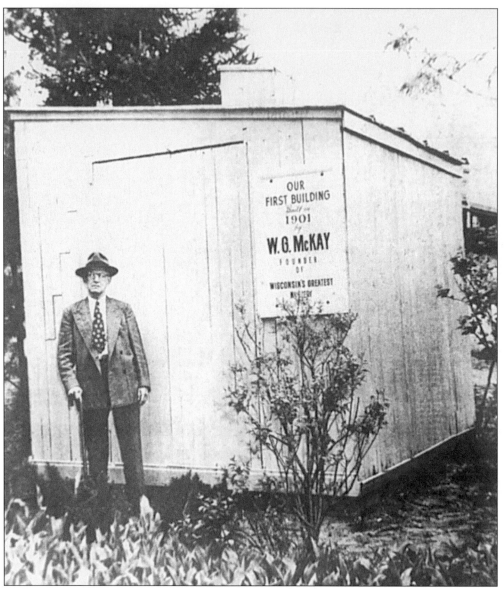
William G. McKay, founder of the McKay Nursery Company, is shown standing in front of the first building. The McKay Company is one of Wisconsin's largest nurseries.

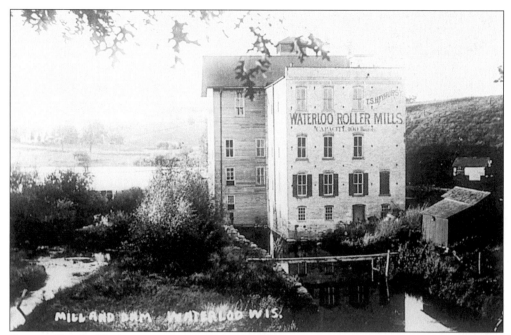

Operated by the Hayhurst family, the Waterloo Roller Mills was the forerunner of the Waterloo Malting Company and one of the city's leading industries up to the beginning of World War I.

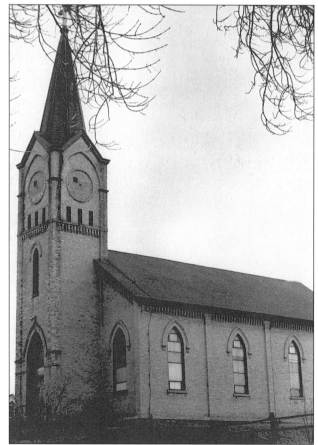

St. Joseph's Catholic Church was founded in Waterloo in 1867. It remained in this building until the 1960s, when a larger church and modern school were built. Since the 1970s, this has been the home of the Waterloo Area Historical Society.

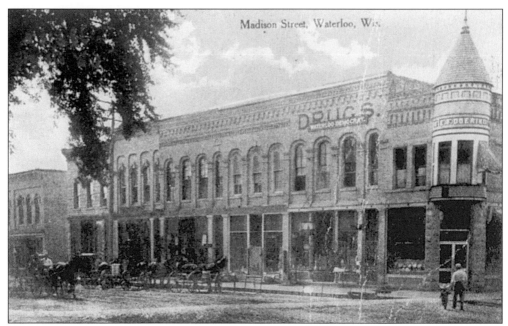

This section of Madison Street in Waterloo shows where the *Waterloo Democrat* was located. Currently, the official city newspaper is the *Waterloo Courier*, which is published on a weekly basis.

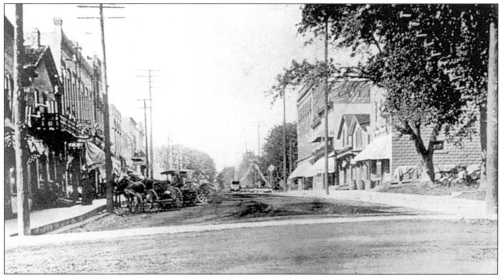

Monroe Street in Waterloo is pictured here shortly after the turn of the century. The building on the right is the current home of the *Waterloo Courier*.

Ten
WATERTOWN

The City of Watertown was founded in 1836 by Timothy Johnson, a carpenter from Connecticut who came here looking for likely places to settle. He named this place "Johnson's Rapids," owing to the tremendous rapids that were apparent in the undammed Rock River that flows through this area.

Johnson laid claim to all of the land that now encompasses the city, and in 1837, the first mill and dam were erected within the site of the future city. The first hotel opened in 1840, and this was followed by the first general store, which opened in 1841.

Settlers, mainly from New England at first, began to pour into the settlement, attracted by the abundant stands of forest for building purposes and the fine water power. The first foreign settlers, Irish and Germans, began to arrive in the mid-1840s.

The name of the settlement was changed to Watertown in 1839 in homage to Watertown, New York, where many of the early settlers came from. The first town meeting was held in 1842. In 1849, Watertown was granted village status and, in 1853, it became a city.

In the 1850s, a plank road was built that linked Watertown to Milwaukee, and in 1855, the railroad came through the city, quickly making it the second largest city in the state with a population of 8,512. Sadly, the depression of 1857 wiped out the railroads and threw the city into a financial panic from which it did not fully recover for nearly 30 years. The population dropped, and it wouldn't be until the 1930s that Watertown would claim 10,000 residents. Today, the city has a population of nearly 21,000, making it the largest city in Jefferson County.

Prominent citizens have included Carl Schurz, the famous German-American politician. His wife founded the first kindergarten in the United States in Watertown in 1856. In addition, Watertown was home to Joseph E. Davies, ambassador to Russia under President Franklin D. Roosevelt, and to Ralph David Blumenfeld, editor of the *London Daily Express*.

Businesses that have flourished in Watertown over the years are numerous. They have included brewing, cigar making, milling, the manufacturing of cutlery, and also the noodling of geese. Currently, businesses in Watertown run the gamut from metal fabrication to digital instruments.

The city enjoys an annual event called Riverfest, which attracts thousands of people from the surrounding areas. With all of this to offer, it is no wonder that the city's motto is "We like it here."

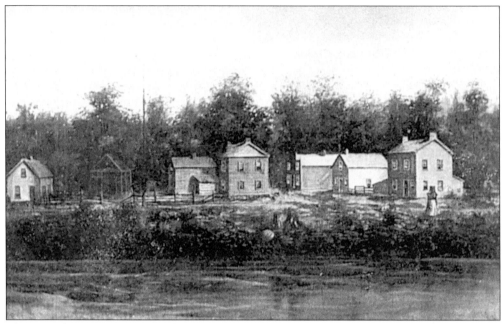

This view shows Watertown in the year 1842. The original of this is a painting in the collection of the Watertown Historical Society.

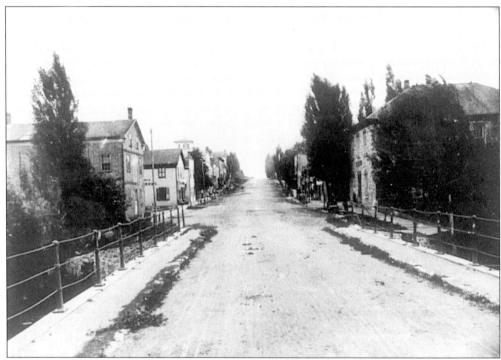

This is perhaps the earliest known photograph of Watertown. It shows Main Street, looking to the west, and dates to about 1853. Note the Rock River House on the right, a popular German hotel, and St. Bernard's Catholic Church, which can just be seen in the distance on the left-hand side of the street.

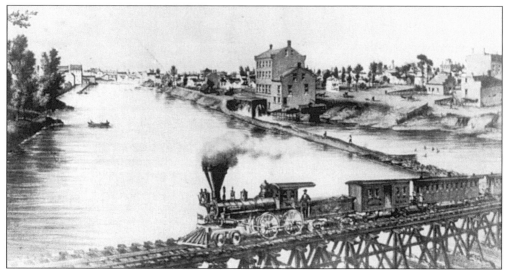

The railroad came through Watertown in 1855, making the city one of the leading centers of commerce and the second largest city in the state. When the railroad was wiped out in 1857, the city was thrown into a financial panic from which it wouldn't recover until the 1880s. This view shows the railroad trestle that still stands below what is today Milwaukee Street. Note the mill in the distance on the right. Today, this is the site of the city water department.

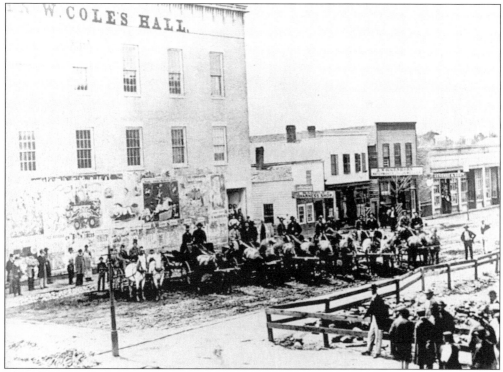

This photo shows "Fair Day," or Cattle Fair, which has been held monthly since 1860. Farmers in the area would bring their animals to trade and sell, though today this is mainly a venue for small items and produce. This photo shows a cattle fair at the intersection of Main and South Second Streets in 1866.

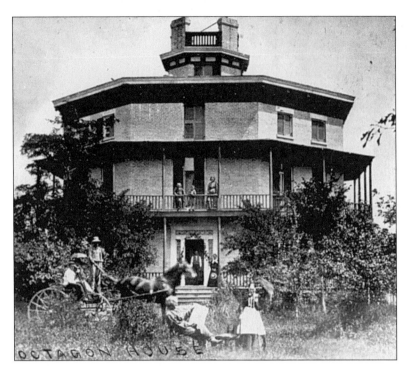

Watertown's historic landmark and museum is the Octagon House. This eight-sided mansion was built in 1854 by John Richards, seen here with his family outside their home. Richards was a lawyer, a mill owner, a farmer, and the mayor of the city.

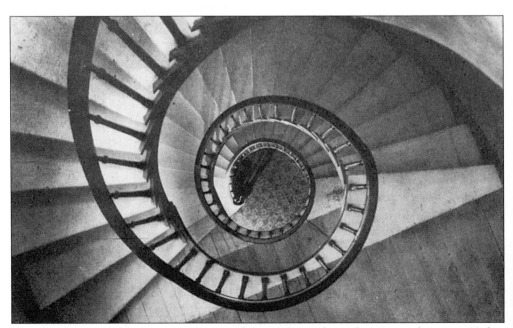

The show piece of the Octagon House is the cantilevered spiral staircase that rises 40 feet through the house. Operated as a museum since 1938, the Octagon House is open to the public on a daily basis from May to November.

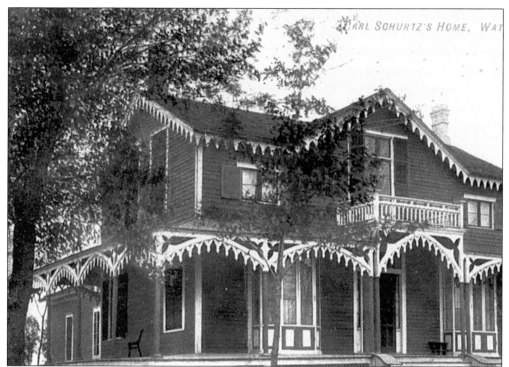

This was the home of Carl Schurz in Watertown. Schurz was a famous German-American politician, who served as an ambassador to Spain under President Lincoln and later as the secretary of the interior under President Rutherford B. Hayes. This house burned down in 1912, and today, a bed and breakfast is on this site.

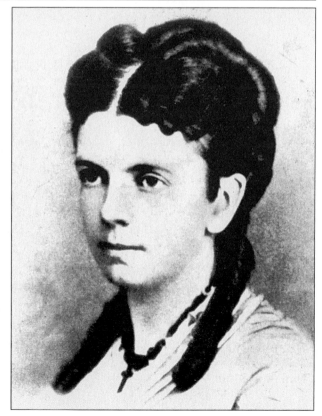

Margarethe Meyer Schurz, wife of the politician Carl Schurz, was the founder of the first kindergarten in America. She based her kindergarten on the teachings of Friedrich Froebel and founded her school in Watertown in 1856. Today, the school is a museum located on the grounds of the Octagon House museum.

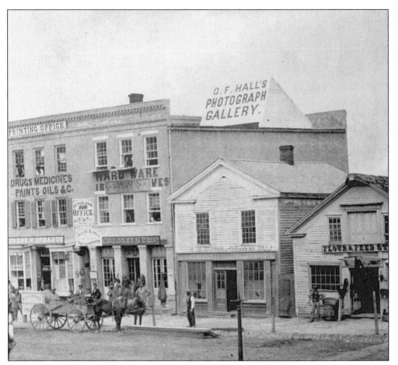

Downtown Watertown in 1866 still had dirt streets and frame buildings. The shop on the far right was one of the first stores in Watertown.

Watertown's first hotel opened in 1840. It was followed by a second hotel in 1843, and by the 1860s there were ten hotels catering to Watertown's citizens. This is the Lindon House, and it was one of the better hotels, having, among other things, a canopied walkway to the outhouse. The hotel burned down in the 1890s and is today the site of the Watertown Public Library.

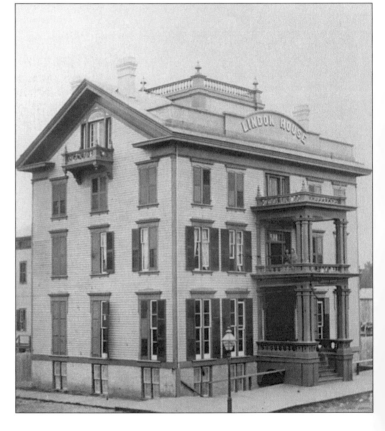

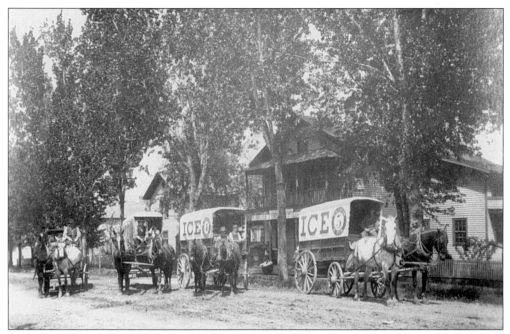

The ice business began in the 1870s when S.M. Eaton started cutting and storing ice. The ice was cut from the Rock River and stored in icehouses along the river. This is S.M. Eaton's soda water factory, called the Badger State Bottling Co., in the 1890s. The ice business would last in Watertown through the 1930s.

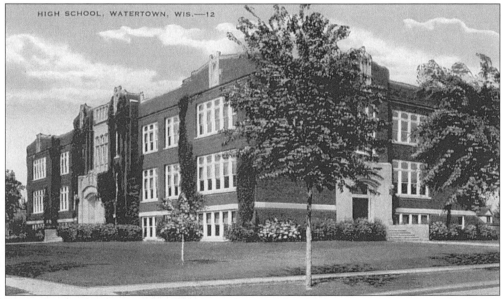

Watertown Senior High School was located on South Eighth Street in Watertown from 1917 until 1994, when a new high school was built. This structure then became an athletic center and pre-school until it was razed in 1999. This was the fourth high school building in Watertown. The first was a small building on the corner of Fifth and Jones Streets in the 1860s, the second was located along Western Avenue in the 1880s, and the third was on Main Street from the 1890s until the erection of this building.

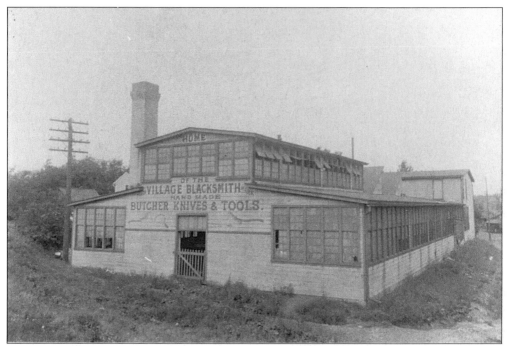

The Village Blacksmith Co. was a leading producer of cutlery and farm implements and tools. Originally called the Washington Cutlery Co., the firm began in Watertown in the early 1900s. It went out of business in the 1970s, and today, it is known as Fisher-Barton.

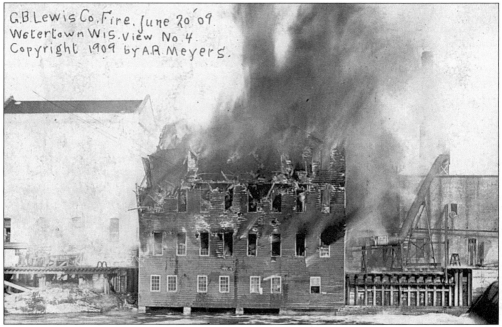

One of the greatest fires in Watertown's history began on the morning of June 20, 1909. The G.B. Lewis Co., a maker of wooden boxes and beeware supplies, caught fire and burned to the ground in a spectacular blaze. The firm later rebuilt in another section of town and, in later years, specialized in fiberglass products.

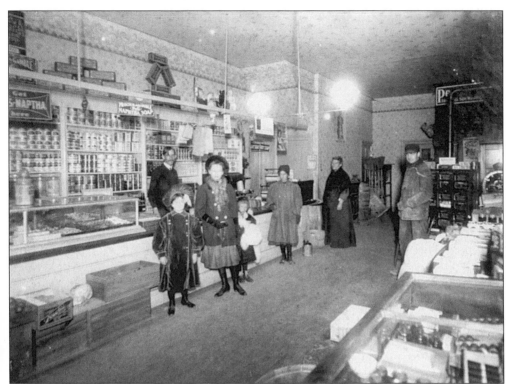

The Nowack grocery was on North Fourth Street in Watertown. At one time, Watertown, like so many other places, had many corner groceries. But with the advent of supermarkets, these little groceries dwindled and died, one of the last of them being the Boyum Grocery, which closed in the late 1970s.

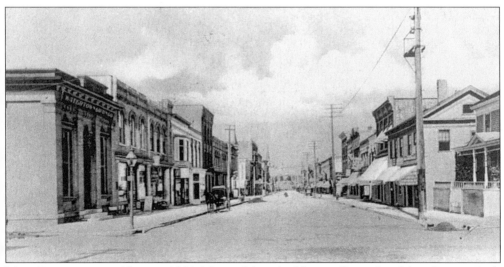

Main Street is pictured here in 1904. Many of these buildings still stand on Main Street, which is one of the reasons why Watertown has one of the largest historic districts in the state.

Acknowledgments

The author of this work would like to thank the following people and institutions for their assistance in compiling this work:

    The Jefferson County Historic Alliance
    The Lake Mills-Aztalan Historical Society
    The Bark River Woods Historical Society
    The Concord Historical Society
    The Fort Atkinson Historical Society
    The Hoard Historical Museum
    The Jefferson Historical Society
    The Johnson Creek Historical Society
    The Palmyra Historical Society
    The Rome-Sullivan Historical Society
    The Waterloo Area Historical Society
    The Watertown Historical Society
    Cynthia Arbiture
    Sue Hartwick
    Olive Gross
    Mary Tutton
    Barbara Woolover
    Iona Turner
    Viola Adams
    Jean Brawders
    Erna Westphal
    Maryann Gleisner
    Dr. Cheryl Peterson
    Gladys Hoffman
    Kathy Nelson

To anyone I may have forgotten, your contributions are no less important, and I thank you. And a special thank you goes to the citizens of Jefferson County, Wisconsin, past, present, and future.